Romiette and Julio

Books by Sharon M. Draper

Tears of a Tiger
Forged by Fire
Darkness Before Dawn
Romiette and Julio

Sharon M. Draper

Romiette and Julio

Simon Pulse

New York   London   Toronto   Sydney   Singapore

First Aladdin Paperbacks edition April 2001

Copyright © 1999 by Sharon M. Draper

Aladdin Paperbacks
An imprint of Simon & Schuster
Children's Publishing Division
1230 Avenue of the Americas
New York, NY 10020

Also available in an Atheneum Books
for Young Readers hardcover edition.

Designed by Lisa Vega.

The text for this book was set in Bembo.
Printed and bound in the United States of America
30 29 28 27 26
The Library of Congress has cataloged the hardcover edition as follows:
Draper, Sharon M. (Sharon Mills)
Romiette and Julio / by Sharon M. Draper.—1st ed.
p.   cm.
Summary: Romiette, an African-American girl, and Julio,
a Hispanic boy, discover that they attend the same high school after
falling in love on the Internet, but are harassed by a gang whose
members object to their interracial dating.
ISBN-13: 978-0-689-82180-6 (hc.)
ISBN-10: 0-689-82180-8 (hc.)
[1. Internet (Computer network)—Fiction. 2. Gangs—Fiction. 3. High
Schools—Fiction. 4. Schools—Fiction. 5. Hispanic Americans—Fiction.
6. Afro-Americans—Fiction.] I. Title. II. Title: Romiette and Julio.
PZ7.D78325Ro 1999 [Fic]—dc21 98-50218
ISBN-13: 978-0-689-84209-2 (pbk.)
ISBN-10: 0-689-84209-0 (pbk.)

To Larry, who gave me the idea
—S.M.D.

Romiette and Julio

1.

Fear

The water thundered into her ears, forced itself down her throat, and burned its way into her nose, her lungs, her brain. This water was fierce and deadly—no cool, gentle waves, but hot, choking liquid flames, sucking the breath of life from her. She struggled, searching for air, for land, for something to hold on to. But there was only the water, pulling her into its depths. She couldn't breathe. She couldn't swim. She couldn't even scream. The water filled her, seared her thoughts, and she drifted slowly into unconsciousness. The fire cooled, the terror ebbed, and the dark shadow of death embraced her.

She drifted then—in a haze of colors and swirls and black, frightening void. Voices? Could she hear voices? One voice? Maybe it was a song. No, all was silence. Thick, enveloping quiet that led to despair. No reason to care, to breathe, to live. So easy to let the silence swallow her. That voice. It pierced the darkness. It was calling her name, grabbing her thoughts and making her remember the fear, the pain, the cold, clammy water. The water! She gasped, and the water grabbed her once more, viciously dragging her to its depths. But that voice. A man's voice. It floated down to where she lay, cradled in the arms of the victorious water. The voice called her one last time.

Suddenly, Romiette sat up in her bed. Her night-gown was damp and clinging to her body. She was sweaty and disoriented. Her heart, still pounding from the fear of almost drowning, made her breathing jagged and tight in the darkness. She turned on her light, looked around her pale blue bedroom, and started to relax. She got up quietly, changed her nightgown, then opened her bedroom window. The night air was cool and soft; peace and silence ruled the street. No cars, no movement, not even a barking dog. Slowly, Romiette began to breathe more evenly. She took a deep breath of the night.

This was the third night in a row that she had been awakened by a dream of drowning, but she had been dreaming various versions of this dream for several months. She could find no reason for such a dream. True, she couldn't swim, but she wasn't taking swimming at school, and she purposely made her life tiptoe far around anything having to do with more water than a bathtub. *So why the terror dream?* she thought again. *Why? And who did that voice belong to?* She could hear it still, and it made her tremble, not with fear, but with excitement. It was not a voice she had heard before—she was sure of that.

It was 3 A.M. Romiette knew she couldn't get back to sleep, so she decided to write in her journal. Writing soothed her, relaxed her, and tonight, she thought, was one of those nights that she needed to really chill. *This was my favorite Christmas present,* thought Romiette as she stroked the smooth leather cover of her new journal.

She sat cross-legged on her bed with a blanket around her shoulders, relaxed a bit, breathed deeply, and opened the journal slowly. She carefully wrote her name on the soft cream-colored front page. She blew on it gently to make sure it would not smear, then, with great anticipation, opened to the first page. She liked starting a fresh journal. It was full of possibilities and unanswered questions—of days yet to come and events yet to happen. She decided to start by describing who she was. Maybe somehow she'd find an answer to the terrible dreams.

2.

Romiette's Journal

My name is Romiette Renee Cappelle. I am brown, like the earth, tall and slim like a poplar tree, and outspoken, like the wind on a stormy day. I like mornings because of all the possibilities, and rainbows when I can find them. I am sixteen years old and I'll be driving by the end of the year.

I like chili, macadamia nut cookies, and environmentally safe products. I believe recycling is essential for the future of this planet, so I never throw anything away. In my room, I have collections of buttons, pop-tops, foil, and safety pins. I like to talk on the phone in the dark because it adds mystery and conserves energy.

I hate picky people, watermelon, and chocolate. I hate gangs, violence, and movies with too much sex and cussing. There are gangs in our school now, and it's a little scary because they want to control with threats and punches the actions and thinking of kids, and

I can't be bothered with that, so they don't like me much. That's fine with me—I don't need any more complications in my life. It's complicated enough trying to juggle geometry, boys, and learning to drive.

I'm not afraid of much. Lots of girls see spiders and snakes and scream. I think snakes are sleek and sexy—not that I'd want to marry one or anything, but I like snakes because they're smooth and cool, and spiders because they create art out of their own bodies. That's awesome. Most spiders don't bite, and if I see one, I go around it rather than step on it. Life is rough enough for a spider without looking out for girls with big shoes. And I do love big shoes. The bigger the better. Three-inch heels and soles. Four inches. Five! My mother said she wore shoes just like those when she was my age. I find that hard to believe. The only other things I'm afraid of are being abandoned, thunderstorms, and water.

I'm terrified of water. I took swimming when I was little like everyone else, but I never learned. That's not exactly true. I learned **how** to swim, I just never got the nerve to let go. I know how to do rhythmic breathing, proper arm strokes, the flutter kick—all of that, but I just can't get away from the side of the pool. When I'm in the middle with nothing to hold on to, I panic. There's just nothing solid—nothing to grasp. The water slips through my hands, and I flounder, then I start to sink, then I scream, then, of course, I get embarrassed. So I go to the pool, but I stay on the side, or splash with the little kids in the shallow end so their parents can go swim in the deep water. Even **walking** by the deep end makes me feel ill. But I've never fallen in, never had a near-drowning incident, never even slipped in the bathtub. Which is why that dream freaks me out. I'm going to have to ask my dad. He would tell me what to do without getting too worried about it.

My daddy, Cornell Cappelle, is a television newscaster. He's good-looking and popular, and his picture is on billboards all over the city. I like that. He gets to interview all the stars and dignitaries that come to town. I got to meet Michael Jackson **and** Michael Jordan last year because of my dad's job. His show comes on every night at six o'clock with this really goofy lady named Nannette Norris. She's pretty, but she can't read very well and keeps mispronouncing words and making stupid mistakes on the air. She once spent the whole show talking about the gorillas in some war in Europe. My dad just smiled, and explained to the listening audience that the guerrilla, not gorilla, warfare was making the war so intense.

My daddy's folk come from New Orleans, and we visit every summer with my grandmama

Essie and my grandpapa Rudolph. Essie makes the best red beans and rice this side of the Mississippi River, and Rudolph tells me tall tales of ghosts and voodoo and stuff my daddy did when he was little. I bet Grandpapa Rudolph would know why I'm having scary dreams about drowning. Grandmama would say it was something I ate, or growing pains, but Grandpapa would light a candle and whisper a tale of a drowned sailor woman and I wouldn't sleep for a week. He'd laugh about it later, but then he'd wink at me and I never could be sure when he was joking or when he really believed what he said.

My mother's name is Lady. I think black folk have the most creative names for their children. We don't bother with ordinary names like Sandy and Mary. We like flamboyant names like LaShandra and LaMarietta or Quinesia or Appolinia. Each name is distinct and descriptive. Anyway, my mama, Lady Brianna Cappelle, is from Cincinnati, where I grew up. Her parents are strict, churchgoing, hymn-singing college teachers who taught me to love music and reading and God. They named their only daughter Lady because that is what they expected her to grow up to be— not a woman, but a lady. And she is. She is six feet tall, with very short dark hair, dark skin, and a figure better than mine, and I'm sixteen and supposedly at the prime of my life. She was a model when she was younger. She walks like an African queen. Grandpa told me that we are direct descendants of African kings, and when I see my mama walk, I believe him.

She never frowns, never yells, and never loses her cool like I do all the time. Once we were shopping and the saleslady started to wait on these teenagers who had come in at least twenty minutes after us. Mama didn't raise a fuss. She said quietly, with that powerful, musical voice of hers, "Excuse me, madam, but the reports of my invisibility have been greatly exaggerated. I'm sure you never intended to overlook my six-foot body and the hundred dollars' worth of merchandise I am holding in my hand." The lady mumbled apologies, Mama smiled sweetly, and we walked out of there like royalty.

My mother owns a boutique downtown. She sells African artifacts and cloth, and imported items from all over the world. She also carries prints from black artists, and lots of books for children and adults by black writers. Anybody who wants a unique outfit or some authentic African artwork, they know to come to Lady Brianna's Boutique. I work there three days a week after school, and most Saturdays. It's not like a job to me, because I love being there. I've read all the latest books, and I've got some really sharp outfits that my friends all admire. People from all over the world come to Mama's shop. Her shop is right between two large hotels, so we love tourists. A couple of times, we've even had visiting kings and presidents of African countries come in. She, the queenly person that she is, was simply charming to them. They appreciated her style and bought lots of stuff.

I like being connected to royalty. I'm tall like my mom, but not tall enough to have that queenly walk. She says it will come later, but I don't know—I may be doomed to walk like a jock all my life. I tried modeling for a while, but I felt stupid grinning when I wasn't happy, and walking when I'd rather be sitting down. Last year I played basketball on a team of girls from my neighborhood. We could beat most of the boys we know, but the boys would never admit it. I don't have a boyfriend and I don't want one. Boys are smelly, noisy, and confusing. They call you and tell you they like you, then they don't call back. They like to act macho, and don't like a girl who is smarter or tougher than they are.

I'd like to find a guy who could talk to me about more than the latest singing group or the scores of last night's game. I want a boy who wonders about life on other planets or if there ever was a continent called Atlantis. I'd like to be able to talk to him about adopting children or the World Wide Web or whether there's a Heaven and a Hell. I want a boy I could tell my dreams to and he wouldn't laugh. He'd understand my fear. I want a boy who would go see a play or a ballet, not just a hockey game or a car show. I believe a relationship should be well balanced. But boys who are smart, good-looking thinkers, if they go to my school, they're hiding from me. I don't think I look too bad, but nobody has seemed to notice yet.

I have soft brown skin, dark brown hair, and light brown eyes like my dad. My favorite color is orange because I think I look good in it. I've got a big smile and even, white teeth that my dad paid a whole lot of money for when I got my braces at twelve. I like school and make good grades most of the time. I have a computer, which really helps my homework look good, and I have friends who I talk to regularly on the Internet. My parents love me, my friends think I'm OK, and I like myself most of the time.

Just as Romiette closed her journal, the alarm clock sliced the silence. It was 6 A.M., and time to get up for school. All of a sudden she was really sleepy, and sorry she had missed two hours of sleep. She sighed, glanced at her pillow, put the journal away under her mattress, and headed to the bathroom for a shower.

3.

Early Morning

It was the first day back after Christmas vacation. The weather was cold—high about twenty, the weatherman said, and snow was predicted. Romiette hoped it would snow all day and all night, enough to call school off for tomorrow. Not likely, she thought, but even after a two-week break, the prospect of an unexpected free day looked great. Romi wore her new pale yellow sweats and shoes, and knew she looked good. She was a little sleepy, but she had grabbed a cup of coffee and a doughnut on the way to school, which she figured would get her through the day.

She entered the front hall, still sipping the last of her coffee. Kids were crowded into the hall, trying to escape the cold, waiting for the bell to ring. Everyone was laughing and joking, comparing new shoes that had been Christmas presents, and talking about the parties and the big basketball game from last week. Romiette had known many of these kids since kindergarten, and she felt comfortable and accepted in the crowd. Destiny, Romi's best friend, dressed in bright pink sweats (they had planned their outfits last night on the phone), her hair newly braided, yelled all the way across the hall, "Hey, Romi! Girls in the house!"

"Hey, Destiny—what's my 'scope for the day?" Destiny did everyone's horoscope and sun signs. She really believed that the stars control the lives of everyone and she did *nothing* without consulting one of the many books she carried for reference. Some of the girls asked Destiny to do a chart for a boy they liked, and even though half of them didn't really believe it all, it was fun, and it was better than just guessing what he might be like.

"Looks good for you, girlfriend. New man coming into your life, but you won't know it for a while."

"Well, I guess I better get rid of the old one first. Marcus, you're outta my life, as of this morning. Destiny has spoken."

"I wish I hadda known I was your man. I woulda taken advantage of it, for sure."

"Yeah, I bet you woulda tried! See, that's why I never told you."

"My heart is broke to pieces! I guess I'm gonna have to keep my girl Ebony here. You the one, girl!" Marcus bowed with fake respect.

"You better watch it, Marcus! Playin' games right in front of my face!" Ebony complained.

"Aw, you know I was just teasin'! You my sweet little Ebony treat. I could just pick you up and sling you to those stars that Destiny be talkin' about all the time!"

"Put me down, Marcus!"

She screamed like she was about to die, but she was laughing, and everyone knew she loved the attention. Destiny and Romiette laughed; they'd both known Marcus and Ebony since fifth grade. They got ready to head to their lockers then, planning to meet again at lunch. Both girls were juniors, but they had very few classes together. Only English with Miss Berry. It was a big school, with about five hundred in each class, so they felt lucky to have lockers close together and one class to share.

"I got something to tell you, Destiny," Romi confided.

"What's up, girl?" Destiny was instantly interested.

"I've been having this dream. . . ."

"The same dream every night?"

"Yeah, almost," admitted Romi.

"Ooo, I love it! Dreams aren't my specialty, but I got this book. . . ."

"I knew you would."

"What's it about? Trains? That means you're gonna travel. Bridges mean you have a decision to make. And bears mean, well, that means you're scared of bears!" Destiny declared.

"No, this one is really scary," Romi said quietly.

"Tell me."

"In the dream, I'm drowning," Romi began. "In deep water, like almost dying. It's terrible, and I'm almost afraid to go to sleep."

"Anything else?" Destiny's eyes were intent.

"Yeah, the water is so cold, it's hot."

"That doesn't make sense!"

"Dreams aren't supposed to make sense! And I'm choking and almost dead, then there's this voice. . . ." It was getting difficult for Romi to tell her friend all of this. It was hard enough to experience, but to say it out loud made it more real and much more frightening.

"Whose voice? Mine?"

"No, it's a male voice. A voice I've never heard before. Not my dad's. Not any dude from around here."

"I like it! Does he save you?" Destiny was intrigued now.

"I don't know. I always wake up just as I hear his voice. Is it true that if you dream you die, then you wake up dead?" Romi asked quietly.

"You mean that you really will die? I've heard that, but nobody who ever died got to come back and tell! Tell me more."

Romi sighed. "I wish I could. That's all I know, but I'm not sleeping very well and I'm getting scared."

"Well, didn't your horoscope say a new man was coming into your life? Maybe you're hearing his voice." Destiny was trying to be helpful.

"I don't know, but something's got to give soon. I don't like this," admitted Romi.

Just then, the bell rang for first period, and somebody yelled, "Fight! Fight! Two dudes is goin' at it!" Dozens of kids rushed to the side of the front hall near the door. Romiette sighed and looked at Destiny. They gave each other a bored shrug, and declared at the same time, "Boys." Romiette never even glanced toward the crowd that surrounded a kid with green hair and a new boy that nobody had seen before.

4.

Julio

He was tall. He was strong. He was angry. And he wasn't afraid to fight. Julio strode down the streets of Cincinnati on that January day, coat collar not doing much to cover his ears from the twenty-degree winds, boots unlaced, fists thrust into his pockets, numbed from the cold. The only thing that kept him warm was his anger. Anger at his parents for bringing him to this cold, gray city. Anger at the sky for being harsh and uncaring. Anger at himself for being scared and shivering in this ugly place. If somebody, anybody, had spoken to him then, he might have lashed out to release his fury. He wanted to destroy a wall or the sky.

But the sidewalk was empty that January morning. Everyone with sense was on a bus or in a car, or inside a heated building. But the bus he thought he was supposed to take never arrived, so after thirty minutes of freezing in the winter wind, he started walking. The school was three or four miles down the road, he figured, so using his anger as a cloak, he headed down the street to a school he had never seen, in a city he had just moved to, to enroll for classes in the second semester of the eleventh grade.

Julio had just moved from Corpus Christi, Texas. He hated Cincinnati with a passion. To Julio, it was cold and dreary and everything seemed to be gray. There was dirty snow all over the dirty sidewalks. *Everything seems tight and enclosed, like nobody breathes here,* he thought. *I want to throw paint everywhere out my window and color this place up! They expect me to LIVE here? Do these people ever have any fun? Not likely. I bet you can't even get a good enchilada here.* As he walked, his toes losing their feeling inside his boots, he glanced at the few barren, black trees that lined the street. Mostly he saw fast-food places and liquor stores next to storefront churches. Piles of trash to be collected. Recycling bins with beer bottles and unread newspapers. A few pigeons. His mood grew darker.

There are no big, sweeping magnolia trees, thought Julio, *only runty little maple trees with cold, skinny branches, no leaves—all naked and stupid-looking. The river here is dirty and dull, not like the beautiful Nueces River, where I learned to swim and sail and fish. Papa said something about going fishing on the Ohio River in the spring. Not me! Probably just catch some old beer cans. No fish with any sense would live in that nasty water!*

He had seen the Ohio River as he and his family flew in over the city. It was brown and thick, and looked more like oozing mud to Julio than refreshing water. He could not imagine why anyone would want to swim in such filth.

Julio loved to swim. He probably learned to swim before he could walk. Water was like his second skin, soothing and relaxing after a hot day in Texas. He was on a swim team once, and the coach tried to get him to think about training for the Olympics, but he figured it would take the fun out of swimming. He also liked to sail with his uncle on his boat. He was a good sailor, and had been planning to buy a little sailboat of his own next year. Sailboat races were held every Wednesday, and last year Julio had won in the junior division. Kids in Corpus Christi get boats instead of cars when they turn sixteen.

Thinking about home made his anger return. Right there on the Gulf of Mexico, swimming and boating were second nature to him. But all that was gone. Nothing remained but cold and bitterness. No soft, warm ocean air, no soft Hispanic flavor here. Just about everybody in Corpus Christi spoke English and Spanish fluently. Most of the people there had relatives in Mexico, across the Rio Grande. The music on the radio, the conversations on the bus, even the breezes that blew there had Spanish melodies floating from them. Here, everything was different. Julio muttered to himself, "May as well have *No habla español!* posted in large *gray* (of course) letters on every dull brown building here."

He had called his friend Diego the night before. Diego had just come in from playing soccer. It was seventy-one degrees back home in Texas. Julio gritted his teeth.

"Hey, Diego, *mi amigo, ¿qué pasa?* What's up?" Julio

could almost feel the Texas breeze over the phone. He sighed.

"*De nada,* Julio. How's Cincinnati?" Diego was slurping on a Popsicle. "Ain't no fun here anymore since you left, man!"

"I hate it here, man. Just 'cause my dad lost his job, I gotta move a million miles from my home so he can start over. It's just not fair!"

Diego had heard Julio complain about this many times. Lots of kids had parents who were suddenly out of work. Several factories had moved out of town, and places like the insurance company that Julio's dad worked for had to cut back because folks just couldn't make the payments. Diego's dad had been out of work for five years. "Stuff is rough, man."

"I hear you!" Suddenly Julio thought about how rough life was for Diego and he was sorry he had complained so loudly. Diego had six sisters, lived in a small apartment, and his mom watched three-year-olds to make ends meet. There was never anyplace to sit or have a moment of silence. That's how they had become friends. Julio's house was cool and quiet. Diego used to come just to "breathe in some silence," he always said. Julio, on the other hand, loved to go to Diego's place because two of his sisters were "really fine." Diego didn't think so, but Julio liked to hang around just to see them brush their hair or laugh on the phone. He even took Maria to the movies once or twice. "How're your sisters?" Julio asked then.

"Angelina is getting married next year. They got engaged at Christmastime. I'll still have five left here, though. I *never* get in the bathroom! That's why I hate you moved, Julio. You had such a nice bathroom!"

"Glad you appreciate the finer things of life, man." Julio grinned.

"What's it like there? Is it like Corpus Christi?" asked Diego.

"Not even close. Bunch of taco fast-food stores— that's about it—and that stuff all tastes like cardboard. And a bunch of ugly buildings that all look like cardboard." Julio sighed again, remembering how homesick he was.

"Do the gray buildings there in Ohio have gang stuff scribbled all over them like here?" Diego knew the other reason that Julio's family moved to Cincinnati was because of the crime and the gangs at their school in Texas. Gang members in their colors roamed the halls, threatening kids and roughing up anybody who opposed them. Fights between the two rival gangs broke out every day.

"Who cares? Gangs are gonna be everywhere, Diego."

"It's getting worse, man. During Christmas break they spray-painted graffiti all over the walls—even in the classrooms. The teachers and principal can't seem to stop them!"

"I'm not surprised. You know, even if the graffiti is cleaned off and painted away, by next week it'll probably be back."

"Now you're gone, Julio, I'm one of the few who still

ain't in no gang. It's hard being out here by myself! I can't ride the school bus or eat lunch in the cafeteria."

Julio and Diego were talking about the unspoken law. They had to eat lunch every day on the steps, try not to act scared, walk home the long way. Either you were in a gang, or you were nobody. It was hard to concentrate on schoolwork with fights in the hall every day and bullies in colors pushing everyone around.

"Yeah, I feel you, Diego. I guess I'm glad I got out of there, but why Ohio? The Montague family has lived in Texas for two hundred years."

"I'm gonna miss those barbecues and weddings at your grandpa's ranch with all your uncles and their wives and kids. Your grandpa is a trip! Doesn't he get married every five years?"

Julio laughed. "Mama says Granpa's a rascal. Papa says he's just trying to recapture his youth. Granpa told me that after his first wife died, he was broken-hearted. He says he's trying to find a woman who can keep up with him! I really miss him already. Just before we left, he told me to keep the river in my heart and follow it."

"Old people say strange things sometimes. You met any girls yet, Julio?"

"I've seen little kids, and old people. Not even any ugly girls. I hate this place! Did I say that already?"

"*Sí*, man. What about school?"

"Don't know. I start tomorrow, but I'm not expecting much. Hey, my mama's calling me. Good to talk to a familiar voice, man."

"Hang in there, Julio. Maybe something good will come outta all this."

"I ain't gonna hold my breath waiting. Later."

Julio could see the school about a block ahead. It was as he expected—tall, brown, and ugly. Schools in Texas were sprawled out over several buildings with walkways and arches and cool breezes. Lunch was always outside, and an air of freedom blew through the whole place. *How will I ever find my way through that giant jail?* Julio wondered bitterly. He walked up to the front of it and tried not to stare. It must have been five stories tall, of heavy brown brick, built to withstand tornadoes and snowstorms. Just looking at the unblinking face of that school made Julio remember how angry he was. He just frowned and walked up the icy front steps to the huge front doors.

The school was dark inside. It even smelled damp and depressing. Julio thought, *I will* never *feel right here!* Kids were gathering in small groups in the front hall, girls giggling, guys laughing too loud. It was January, the first day back after Christmas vacation, and everyone was excited to see their friends after two weeks away. No one noticed or spoke to Julio. One girl squealed shrilly as a boy picked her up and lifted her over his head. She yelled, "Put me down, Marcus!" but you could tell she was enjoying the attention. Julio stood near the door, watching the friends chatter about nothing and everything, and hating every moment of it. He clenched his fists, and found himself breathing hard. He felt like he was about to explode.

"Hey, man! Get out the way!" A tall, freckled boy wearing two safety pins as earrings, a small gold nose ring, and bright green hair—green like the color of a fluorescent marker—fell through the door where Julio had been standing, and knocked Julio sprawling to the floor. He jumped up and spun around in one swift movement, took his right fist out of his pocket, and all of his anger and frustration exploded in the center of the green-haired boy's face. Bright red blood spurted from his nose, making him look somehow like a leftover Christmas decoration.

"Fight! Fight!" somebody yelled, and instantly a crowd surrounded the two boys. Kids started jostling and pushing, cramming in to see the fight, shoving each other and getting louder in the hot, crowded hallway. The bell rang then, and the principal, large, balding, and red faced, pushed his way through the crowd, which somehow disappeared in seconds.

"What's going on here?" he demanded. "Who started this? Five minutes back in school and you're already fighting. I'm not going to start the new year off with this kind of mess. Both of you in my office right now!" He was sweating heavily and breathing hard.

Ben, the one with green hair, who was now sitting on the floor holding his nose with one hand and his nose ring in the other, had no desire to take on an angry stranger. And Julio was no longer so angry. Too bad this strange, skinny kid got in the way of months of frustration. They looked at each other, then looked at the sweating, red faced principal, and almost grinned. Ben spoke first. "Mr. Prince! Nobody's fighting! This dude here was just trying to help me up. I was running and I slipped on the ice on the front steps and hit my nose on the door. I was thinking of calling my lawyer, or maybe America's Most Wanted, or maybe the president. I think you ought to get some salt on that slippery spot, Mr. Prince. Now if *you* should fall, sir, we might have an earthquake or something, and we wouldn't want that to happen, because that would interrupt our educational success, and since I always wondered how much pressure a nose would have to put on a door to make it bleed, I feel that I have learned something this early morning, even before class starts!"

The principal just shook his head and said, "Shut up, Ben. It's too early in the morning for your babbling." He turned to Julio, who was amazed and trying not to laugh at Ben, who so glibly got him out of trouble. "Young man, is that what happened? Did he slip and fall?"

Julio looked at Ben, who was grinning in spite of a very swollen nose, and replied, "I'm new here, Mr. Prince. Why would I hit someone I don't know? Today is my first day, and I came to enroll. Here are my transcripts from Texas." Mr. Prince didn't believe either of them, but he had morning announcements to make, a sick teacher's class to cover, and a call to make to the custodian to get some salt on the front steps, so since the danger seemed to be over, he let it go.

"Take your stuff to the secretary in Room 102," he told Julio. "And Ben, get to class!" He weighed at least three hundred pounds, and he waddled as he headed down the hall. Ben watched him, put his book bag under his coat, and pretended to huff and sweat and roll. He burst into laughter as soon as Mr. Prince was out of earshot.

Julio echoed his laughter. It felt good to laugh. It was almost as satisfying as that right hook into Ben's nose.

"Why'd you help me?" Julio asked, laughing again. "Why didn't you narc on me? I punched your lights out."

"Well, fortunately, I had a spare set of bulbs and I could see you had some issues that had nothing to do with me. Am I right?"

"Yeah, man. I just got here and nothing was going right and I want to be back home in Texas, and then some kid with green hair knocks me down."

"Hey, tomorrow it will be blue! I like being original! If you ever see me looking ordinary, you got permission to punch me out again. I gotta get to class. What's your name, dude? I gotta know who redecorated my face."

"Julio. I'm Julio Montague."

"I'm Ben! Ben Olsen. Later, dude."

"Later, and thanks."

Julio thought about the incident with Ben as he waited for the secretary with the blue eyeliner to check his papers and give him a class schedule. *I could be getting kicked out of school, instead of checking in,* he thought. *If it had been me getting punched by a crazed stranger, I would have clocked him, not helped him. Amazing dude, that Ben.*

Julio got his schedule, sighed, and headed to the fourth floor for his math class. The halls were mostly empty by now, with crumpled paper and candy wrappers littering the floor. He could hear Mr. Prince's monotone voice making the morning announcements, stuff about SAT registration forms, and tardy slips, and the basketball game tomorrow night. None of it had any meaning for him as he checked all the closed doors in that long, dark hallway but couldn't find Room 407. He saw 405, 406, then the numbers jumped to 412 and 413. *Why do schools do this stuff to kids?* he thought in frustration.

"Yo, Chico, you lost?" The voice came from the end of the hall.

"Yeah, man, and my name's not Chico."

"You look like a Chico to me. Room 407 is around the corner in the new wing . . . Chico."

Julio walked toward him, his anger returning, but the boy disappeared into a classroom. All Julio saw was that he had on purple sweats. Julio was frowning when he walked into 407. That "Chico" comment made him tense and irritated. Anglos at home used that name as a put-down. And, at home, it was mostly the Anglo gang members who used it. This was not a good sign.

The math teacher, a tall, skinny man with a really cheap hairpiece that slid whenever he moved his head and did not match his graying hair, looked at

Julio and smiled. "Welcome, Julio. You can take that seat behind Brandy. Are you a good math student, or will you fit right in with my friends sitting here who think math was invented by beady-eyed monsters?"

Julio grinned. "You mean it wasn't?" he said with mock surprise.

The teacher, Mr. Whitehead, rolled his eyes and smiled again. "Yep, you're going to fit right in here! Here's a textbook. We're on page 155."

Most of the kids ignored Julio. A few of the girls looked him over with interest, but nobody spoke or even smiled. They seemed to pay more attention to the fresh snow that was falling than to the discussion on polynomials. Large, flat flakes floated slowly at first, then thick like falling cloud bits, covering the dirt and grayness of the city. Julio watched also, admiring the beauty of the falling snow, and wishing it could cover all the darkness and fear he felt inside as well.

5.

Destiny and the Scientific Soul Mate System

Destiny ran up the stairs to Romiette's room and barged in without knocking. Romi was used to it. Now that Destiny was driving, she dropped over whenever she felt like it, which was usually once a day and three or four times on the weekend. Destiny's car was bright red, with dozens of brightly colored butterfly decals on it. Instead of looking tacky, though, it looked just perfect for her. She liked the music loud, the convertible top down, even in the coldest weather (just in case the "right" man was looking her way), and a huge bumper sticker that read, PRACTICE RANDOM ACTS OF KINDNESS AND SENSELESS ACTS OF BEAUTY!

"Romiette! Romiette! Just check this out, girl! This is the bomb! Can you lend me forty-five dollars? I've got the answer to your dream problems and my man problems too!"

"Forty-five dollars? You got me bent! What do you need that much money for, Destiny? And how is it going to solve all our problems?"

"I got enough for the shipping and handling. I can't

believe you don't know. Check out page fifty-four."

"Now, if I didn't know you so well, I'd ask page fifty-four of what. But where's the magazine? Is it *Heavy Hunks* or *Teen Scene*? The teen magazine industry would go out of business if Destiny Louise Dodson canceled all her subscriptions!"

"Don't talk so loud! I would *die* if anyone else knew my middle name. How could parents who were cool enough to give me a dynamite name like Destiny give me such a stupid middle name?"

"I thought it was the name of the aunt you like who's the astrologer in California."

"I'm getting my middle name changed when I'm twenty-one—to something like Sagittarius or Karma."

"You're a trip, Destiny." Romi laughed and reached for the magazine. "So what's so special in *Heavy Hunks* this month?"

"You know I just read *Heavy Hunks* for inspiration." Destiny rolled her eyes. "How am I gonna find me the perfect man if I don't know what's out there?"

"Yeah, like we know anybody who looks like the dudes in that magazine. They all got big shoulders, hazel eyes, tight butts, and look like they're 'bout to pop out of those tight turquoise bikini bottoms they dress them in. They all go to Yale, are majoring in medicine, and plan to dedicate the millions they're gonna make to the poor."

"So what's wrong with that?" Destiny asked with a grin.

"You ever seen one *real* dude that looks even close to one of them?" retorted Romi.

"Well, no, but that's why I *look* so hard. When I see him, I'll know. I will see his tight turquoise butt in the distance on the beach—"

"We live in Ohio. Which beach would that be?"

"Quit steppin' on my dream. He will know too. He'll be my soul mate. He will see my slim, supple body, my long, flowing hair, my perfect white teeth—"

"He must have forgotten his glasses then!"

"Now just stop. When I find him, you'll take back all your jokes. My soul mate is out there. I know it. He's searching for me too."

"Reality calling Destiny . . . He's not there yet. What did you find in the magazine that you need forty-five dollars for?"

"Oh! I almost forgot what I wanted to show you. It's called the Scientific Soul Mate System! It's just perfect!"

"You got to be kidding," Romi said with a grin.

"No, for real. You know you believe in soul mates. You just think you're gonna find yours when you're twenty-five. I can't wait that long. I need a date for the prom by June. I gotta find him now! There's nothing that says I can't speed up the process. Check this out. Here's the ad. It's even got my name in it!"

The Scientific Soul Mate System

Do you feel the soul of another calling to you? Do you know in your heart that your destiny and his were meant to merge in the cosmos? We can help you find him.

The Scientific Soul Mate System has been designed to help you find that special someone. The kit includes everything you need.

1. The Dream Wish Candle—Specially scented with the aroma of raspberries, known to enhance dream images. Simply light the candle before you go to sleep, and let the gentle smell of raspberries lead you to the dream of that special someone. (Candles are shipped in a sturdy globe for maximum safety.)

2. The Dream Ointment—Rub just a dab on each temple each evening. Feel the tingle of the peppermint-based salve as it penetrates your consciousness and helps to visualize the dream image.

3. The Dream Tape—Selected instrumental music with rhythms that match the human heartbeat. Play this softly near you as you sleep. The dream of your soul mate is only a heartbeat away.

4. The Dream Journal—Keep this near your bed so that when you awaken in the morning you can capture the dream images before they disappear. Special Dream Pen included at no extra cost.

This $75.00 value can be yours for only $44.99, plus $9.99 for shipping and handling. Rush your order today!

"Romiette, I have *got* to get this!" cried Destiny. "Besides, maybe they will give you some answers to that dream you've been having. Maybe you'll get a face to go with that voice."

"Destiny, you are nuts! You don't really believe this, do you?"

"Look, Romiette, if you lend me the money, you can come over and spend the night, and we'll try it together. It can't hurt. It doesn't work as well if you don't truly believe, though. I'll pay you back next week when my dad gets back from his trip."

"OK, let's try it. You know I just got paid."

"And you got money left over? Girl, it was meant to be! Here's the address. Let's go down to the post office and get a money order. I want to mail this today! Who knows—you may find your soul mate too. Maybe that voice you hear is your soul mate calling out to you."

"I don't need a soul mate yet. I have trouble enough dealing with just me—and keeping up with you!"

"But just suppose . . ."

"Yeah, suppose I dream about *your* soul mate. How are we supposed to know?"

"Gotta read the fine print on the instructions. We'll figure it out. Let's get going—post office closes in an hour."

"I'm with you, girl. But I don't know why." Romi grabbed her purse, and the two headed out to Destiny's car.

6.

Julio at Home

Julio sloshed through the wet and melting snow, up the unshoveled walkway of their apartment building. It wasn't luxurious, nor was it raggedy; it was just so very ordinary. *Generic,* thought Julio. *Just like any other apartment complex in the United States.* He opened the door to the first-floor hallway and the warm smell assaulted him. It wasn't an unpleasant odor, it was simply the shared smell of many people living under one roof—combined smells of food and fights and joy and tears. Julio felt alone in that symphony of odors. He wanted the familiar fragrances of his home in Texas.

Luis Montague, his dad, was trying to clear all the boxes from the living room. He smiled as Julio walked into the room. He was proud of his tall, brooding son, and understood his pain. "So how was your first day at the new school, son?"

"I hate it."

"How can you know? You just got here. Here, help me move these boxes."

"I hate the snow. I hate this city. I hate the kids here. I want to go back home."

"This is our home now, Julio."

"*Sí*, Papa, but I don't have to like it."

"Did you try to make friends today? A smile, perhaps?"

"Papa, nobody in the eleventh grade smiles."

"I know. Terminal depression for a year. It will pass, my son. Give it time. It's difficult for me and your mother as well."

"Not like for me. You got each other. I got nothing. And there's nothing Spanish here in Cincinnati."

"We haven't yet had the chance to investigate all the possibilities. We may be pleasantly surprised. There's the phone, can you get that? My hands are full."

"Yeah, sure, Papa. Hello?"

"May I speak to Julio Montague?"

"You got him."

"This is Ben, the kid with the green hair and the red nose!"

"Hey, Ben, how'd you get my number?"

"I got friends in high places—like my sister who works in the office."

"You know, I sorta looked for you today, but I didn't see any green hair all day," Julio admitted.

"I slipped out early. I used a broken nose as an excuse, but I had to go play in the snow. I need to sled on virgin snow. After school, all the little kids with runny noses will have tramped all over it. I had the whole afternoon on a clean slope of untouched snow. Awesome!"

"Sounds OK, I guess, if you like snow."

"You don't like snow?" Ben asked incredulously.

"Naw, not much. We never got much snow in Corpus Christi. Too wet. Too messy. Too cold. Gets in my shoes and under my shirt."

"But have you ever sledded on virgin snow?" teased Ben.

"I can't say that I have."

"OK, next snowfall, I'll take you and show you the glory of initiating a perfect hill on a cold, clear afternoon. What you doin' tonight?"

"I don't know. Chillin', I guess."

"It's going down to five below tonight. You'll be chillin' all right."

"It never gets this cold in Corpus Christi. My friends at home are out on the river with their sailboats."

"Awesome. You got a boat?"

"Not of my own, but I can use my uncle's any time I want. I'm a good sailor. Maybe as good as you are on a sled. You ever been sailing?" Julio asked.

"No, not really. The only boat I've been on is one of those tour boats on the river."

"Well, if it ever warms up around here and that dirty thing you call a river downtown ever melts, I'll take you on a virgin sailing trip."

"Sounds good to me. I like virgin anything!" Ben chuckled. "So what's it like in Corpus Christi?"

"It's, well, different. Different colors, landscape, feels, smells. It's hard to explain."

"I feel you. It's like me and my hair. Different. What kind of name is Montague anyway? You Spanish or Greek or what?"

"My family is from Mexico, but Montague is an Italian name. Some Italian count, hundreds of years ago, who was running away from trouble with some king, ended up in Mexico, got married there, and it has been our family name ever since."

"That's deep—that you can trace your family back that far. My dad passes through from time to time, so it's just me and my mom and my sister and my jars of hair dye, which I do *not* let my sister use. Mom lets me do what I need to. She's really cool, but I'd never tell her," Ben admitted.

"My parents are great, but uptight. Rules. Manners. Proper ways of doing everything. Family tradition."

"That's gotta be tough. I don't think I even know what's a proper way to do anything."

"Come to my house. My father will let you know," Julio assured him.

"What would he say about my hair?" Ben asked.

"Oh, it would shock his socks off! It would be worth it just to see the expression on his face."

"We're going to have to do that one day. But wait till I make it bright red and put it in spikes!"

"Spikes? How do you do that?" asked Julio.

"It's easy—Elmer's glue! Washes out easy. Freaks out the adults."

Julio laughed. "I like your style, Ben. Maybe you can help me find a job here."

"What you want to do?"

"Anything for extra money, but I'd really like a job at a TV station or something."

"Ladies and gentlemen: Here is the six o'clock

news. Nothing happened today, so tomorrow has been canceled. Film at eleven."

"Ben, you're crazy. No, get me straight now—I don't want to be one of those cheese-grinning reporters—I want to be the man who makes them look good," admitted Julio.

"Nice job, if you like cables and cameras. Then, when you get famous, you can make movies! Lights! Action! Quiet on the set! Montague is making another movie! A nine-hundred-billion-dollar blockbuster!"

"I like your vision, man. Hey, you got E-mail? I did get to bring my computer when we moved. That helps, because I can still talk to a couple of kids through the Internet."

"Yeah, I love it, man! I love making up names and identities and telling strangers trash about me!"

"You make stuff up?" Julio asked incredulously.

"You tell the truth?" Ben responded with the same amount of surprise. Both laughed.

"Yeah, but I don't have to worry about what I look like or what they think of me," Julio added. "I can always erase what I type and do it over or make it right. In real life, there's only one chance to make a good impression."

"But, see, I don't *care* if I make a good impression. Actually, I hope I don't! It's more fun that way!"

"You got spice, man."

"And you got potential, Julio, my friend."

"I hate being the new kid."

"Hang with me, and you won't be new for long. Might ruin your reputation, but since you ain't got one yet, who cares! Gotta go, dude. Check you out tomorrow!"

"Later, Ben. And thanks for calling."

"Is that one of those proper things your parents taught you to do?"

"Yeah, I guess."

"I really gotta work on you!"

"Remember I was the one who worked on you first! How's the nose?"

"Black and blue. I'm dyeing my hair the same color tonight in sympathy! Later!"

"Peace, man."

"So, Julio, was that a friend from school?" Luis asked with interest.

"Just a dude with green hair, Papa."

"Green hair?"

"Only for today. Tomorrow it's gonna be blue."

"I don't understand."

"I know, Papa, but that's cool. I'm gonna go do some homework and maybe get on the computer before I turn in. Need any more help with the boxes?"

"No, I finished while you were on the phone."

"Oh, sorry, Papa. I'll help you more tomorrow."

"Sure. Good night, son. Be sure to say good night to your mother, Julio. She worries about you."

"I know, Papa. I will."

7.

Chat Room

Welcome to TEEN TALK, the best partying chat room on-line! TEEN TALK is open every day, 24 hours a day!

cookieman: hey, gimme your age/sex check

bigmac: HIYA

sweetthing: 16/f

becool: 17/m

afroqueen: 16/f

niobe: 15/f

oogaooga: 14/m

spiceboy: 17/m

afroqueen: whatsup?

bigmac: any girls from Boston here shout YEAH BABY

niobe: who cares?

sweetthing: no one wants to shout it

bigmac: well whisper it then

cookieman: my parents are gone 4 the weekend!!!

niobe: party!!

afroqueen: can I come?

cookieman: yup just find me

becool: I have this gum in my mouth that I have been chewing for five hours and I think I need

spiceboy: lol :-)

becool: to spit it out

niobe: good idea

sweetthing: a boy has been spreading rumors about me at school.

niobe: same here

sweetthing: what did you do?

bigmac: what he said was probably true

afroqueen: just shut up, bigmac. your breath smells like hamburgers!

becool: lol

sweetthing: what did you do, niobe?

niobe: confronted him. told him to drop dead.

sweetthing: did that work?

niobe: he left me alone after that

cookieman: any females here from CO? press 34

vanityfair: I'm from CAL

bigmac: he said CO, stupid

cookieman: CAL will do. what's your shoe size?

vanityfair: why—you planning to buy me some shoes?

cookieman: no, I just hate girls with big feet

bigmac: go kick yourself

spanishlover: who's here?

afroqueen: hey, spanishlover, welcome to the zoo!

sweetthing: nice name, spanishlover, are you all that?

spanishlover: all that and more, sweet-thing!

sweetthing: :-)

afroqueen: state your stuff, spanishlover

spanishlover: 16/m and ready for action

vanityfair: watch out!

niobe: we got metal detectors put in at our school today

bigmac: yeah, everybody and they daddy got one now

afroqueen: I hate that. they treat us like criminals

becool: some of us are!

oogaooga: they do locker searches every week at my school

afroqueen: what they looking for? lunch?

vanityfair: lol :-)

spiceboy: drugs

becool: once they even brought in drug-sniffing dogs

sweetthing: they treat US like dogs

bigmac: they took all our pagers in a sweep once!

niobe: yeah, like we all drug dealers!

cookieman: my mama bought my pager. said that's the only way to keep up with me. she made them give it back.

bigmac: yeah, they finally gave them back to us too. too many.

vanityfair: I hate when they look in my bag and my purse. makes me feel cheap

spiceboy: you ARE cheap!

vanityfair: go bite yourself

afroqueen: they don't ever check the teacher's purse and pockets

sweetthing: yeah, they probably holding

spanishlover: we had gangs at my old school

cookieman: so what else is new?

spiceboy: gangs run everything

afroqueen: no, gangs RUIN everything

oogaooga: yeah, you just put up and shut up

afroqueen: I don't mess with them

spiceboy: you join or you pay or you hide

niobe: you ever seen a gun up close?

becool: yeah, I got one. my old man bought for me.

cookieman: you lie!

vanityfair: what does it look like?

becool: It's black and heavy.

cookieman: you lie! you ain't got no gun.

becool: no lie. he said a man gotta have protection.

afroqueen: you ever shoot it?

becool: yeah, at cans and birds

oogaooga: birds gotta fly, man. don't take it out on birds.

sweetthing: you ever take it to school?

bigmac: only fools do that

becool: yeah, once. in my book bag.

niobe: you get busted?

becool: I'm too slick

spiceboy: you ever see somebody get shot?

becool: no. don't want to

spiceboy: I did once. it was a drive-by in LA.

niobe: who got shot?

spiceboy: some kid—waiting on the bus with his mother

sweetthing: makes me wanna cry

spiceboy: she was screaming and blood was everywhere

afroqueen: did he die?

spiceboy: I don't know. I left.

cookieman: I hate blood

afroqueen: and killing

sweetthing: I hate cows

niobe: cows? why?

sweetthing: I live on a farm

spanishlover: what else do you hate?

becool: dead snakes. live ones are cool.

cookieman: peppermint toothpaste

oogaooga: homework. waste of time.

vanityfair: my mother

sweetthing: dirt, mud, and anything else that's brown and stinky

afroqueen: commercials with athletes who sweat

spiceboy: crank phone calls

niobe: blue eye shadow

spanishlover: gangs

vanityfair: fights

becool: cops

cookieman: guns

sweetthing: bombs

afroqueen: death

niobe: We just read Hamlet in school. EVERY-BODY dies.

becool: who cares?

oogaooga: Shakespeare is stupid.

afroqueen: it's not so bad

spanishlover: you into Shakespeare?

cookieman: Shakespeare was a dude!

niobe: so was Charles Manson—what's your point?

vanityfair: suppose Shakespeare was a woman?

sweetthing: maybe he was

becool: who cares!

bigmac: would we still have to read that stuff in school?

afroqueen: no—cause nobody paid any attention to women back then!

cookieman: nobody pays any attention now.

niobe: you do

cookieman: only for joy, babe—only for joy!

spanishlover: anybody here from Cincinnati?

bigmac: who would WANT to live there?

spanishlover: not me. I just got here and I hate it here

becool: where did you move from?

spanishlover: Texas

sweetthing: I went to Texas once. Too hot!

spanishlover: it's not hot on the river where I lived

afroqueen: what about the Ohio River?

spanishlover: it's ugly!

becool: so is your mama!

spanishlover: my mama uses your mama to clean her shoes!

afroqueen: what you got against the Ohio River?

spanishlover: like I said, it's the ugliest river I've ever seen!

afroqueen: it's winter, what do you expect? the river is muddy. What's it supposed to look like? a blue crayon drawing?

spanishlover: it's not just your river. I hate everything here. it's cold and I want to go home.

afroqueen: you sound unhappy

spanishlover: depressed

bigmac: why don't you two take it to a private chat room?

spanishlover:afroqueen?—see you there?

afroqueen: I'm with you—

8.

Private Chat Room Conversation

Dear Afroqueen:
I'm from Texas. Do chat rooms get on your nerves? There's so much junk! Nobody really says anything, just little one-liners that mean nothing.

Hey, Spanishlover:
Yeah, they annoy me. Some are better than others. I've been in some where we really talked about stuff. So what's so great about Texas?

The Nueces River flows proud and beautiful all year. As does the Rio Grande. It's wide and powerful, and I really miss it. And it never gets cold there like it does here. Does the river ever freeze?

I've never seen the river freeze, and I've lived here all my life. But I've heard that it has frozen before. Boats get stuck right in the middle. I've never seen any other river, though. I figured they all looked the same—kinda wet.

No, there is a difference. Some rivers are heavy and slow, others are cheerful and lively. Just like people.

So are you a deep river or a stagnant stream?

I'm an ocean. I'm real deep. What about you?

Me? I'm a lake. I got edges, but I also have ripples and possibilities. Now, cut all this, and tell me about you really.

Like I said, I'm from Texas. I like Tejano music, refried beans, and guacamole. But I also like pizza, German chocolate cake, and sauerkraut.

Remind me never to have dinner with you. Do you eat the sauerkraut on the pizza or with the German chocolate cake?

Both! Let's see, what else can I tell you about me? I like to sail and I'm a good swimmer. I can play two different instruments and I speak two languages. I hate TV talk shows and stupid billboards. Now, your turn.

Me? I'm one of the only girls in our class who

uses the Internet and talks to people on-line. I like to read, and write poetry, and go to dances, but I also play basketball and soccer. You can sail and swim? I really admire that. I never learned to swim.

I've never met anyone who couldn't swim. Swimming is like breathing. How can you not know how to swim?

Cause when you're swimming, you can't breathe! I've taken lessons since I was three. Couldn't do it. I'm just plain terrified of the water. But I know I'll never drown, unless it's in the bathtub, because I never intend to get close enough to any water that's deeper than that!

I am afraid of being alone, of being abandoned.

I guess most kids feel that. Have you ever been left alone?

No, not even been lost in a grocery store. But fear doesn't make much sense. It is just something you know and respect. Your fear of the water will make you strong.

Maybe, but sometimes my fear takes over. I have bad dreams. Actually, I've been having this one really terrifying dream. . . .

What kind of dream?

Never mind. Can you speak Spanish?

Sí. Of course. My whole family is from Mexico. What about you?

I'm taking French II, but I'd be afraid to go to France with what I know. You know what else I like to eat? French croissants, and grape jelly. Also Cincinnati chili, but not with grape jelly on it! Have you ever tried any of the chili?

No, I haven't had a chance to try Cincinnati chili, with or without jelly. But unless it's hot and spicy, I probably won't like it. My mother uses hot sauce on everything. Now I can't eat a meal without it!

Hot sauce. Yuck. And you had such potential. I bet you like carbonated pop too, don't you? I like mild things—like fresh fruit juice instead of soda pop, and warm gravy instead of hot sauce (except on oatmeal—that gets warm milk, not warm gravy!).

What about music? What's your favorite?

Well, I listen to rock and rap and R&B, but believe it or not, I like classical music sometimes too. It helps me write poetry and relaxes me when I can't sleep. I don't tell many people this. You know my favorite? Mandolin music. I discovered it late one night when I was listening to the radio, feeling moody and blue. It was beautiful.

You're not going to believe this, but I play the mandolin! My grandfather taught me when I was a little boy. And you're right. It's a beautiful sound. But I also play the saxophone. I like the music, but there's not much call for mandolins in the school marching band, not even in Texas.

Give me a break! Nobody plays the mandolin, at least not on purpose! Wow, that's awesome! Hey, I've got to get off of this computer and help my mom with the dishes. Sign on tomorrow at four. Let's talk again. This was cool! Peaceout—Afroqueen

I'll be there! Talk to you then. Peaceout—Spanishlover

9.

Destiny and Romiette

"Girl, that was the best movie I ever saw!" Destiny sighed as the final credits rolled off the screen. She was dabbing her eyes with the edge of the blanket on Romiette's bed. "Rewind it to the part where she has to decide if she's gonna stay with her soul mate, who she loves like hot fire, or her crippled husband, who has loved her with pure, sweet trust since childhood. Ah! The agony of true love!"

"You say that after every love story we rent, Destiny. And get a tissue! You're always crying on my blankets." Romiette hit the remote to rewind the tape, and turned on the lights.

"That's because I'm an expert on love, Romi. I understand the pain of passion."

"You've never even had a boyfriend, except for Jerome in the seventh grade. How do you know so much?" Romi laughed.

"Imagination, girlfriend! I read. I dream. I will know him when he walks through the door." Destiny was walking dramatically across the bedroom just as the downstairs doorbell rang.

"There's the doorbell. It's the pizza. Why don't you answer the door, Destiny, just in case the pizza boy is your secret soul mate." Romi grinned and gave Destiny half the pizza money.

"You got me bent! I've seen the pizza boy. Not a chance!" Destiny ran downstairs to get the pizza, their usual of pineapple and peppers, and returned with the large square box and a soda from Romi's refrigerator. The smell of the warm cheese, spicy sauce, and soft bread filled the room.

"Did the soul mate package come yet, Destiny?" Romi asked between bites.

"No, but I have faith. It'll be here by next weekend. We gotta get a life, Romi. How am I going to get a date for the prom if I spend every weekend looking at videos with you? We need new blood!"

"Speaking of new blood, I met a guy a couple of days ago." Romi waited for a pillow to be tossed at her.

Destiny screamed, "And you're just now telling me? Girl, spill it! I told you my cards said you were going to meet a new man. And you weren't even looking! What does he look like? Is he fine?"

"Well, I don't know. I've never seen him." Romi grinned.

"You talkin' crazy. How did you meet him if you've never seen him?" asked Destiny.

"I've only talked to him on the Internet." Romi waited for Destiny's reaction.

Destiny jumped on the bed and dropped her pizza on the floor. "You met a man on the computer? Girl, that's where serial killers and rapists be hanging out. They make you think they're OK, then they make plans to meet you, then you end up with your picture on the back of a milk carton!"

Romi laughed and picked up the fallen pizza. "He wasn't like that. I don't think he was one of those perverts. He sounded really nice. He seemed real."

"You didn't do anything stupid like give him your real name or something, did you?" Destiny was not going to be convinced so easily. She figured Romi had lost her mind.

"No, of course not. I'm not stupid. But he did seem really sincere."

Destiny spent quite a bit of time on the Internet herself. It was her opinion that the whole Web was full of freaks waiting to find her and attack. "You better be careful, girl. Those sex stalkers on the Internet know exactly what to say to make you think they're the same age as you are. Did he say anything about sex or freaky stuff?"

"No, not at all. But, now that you mention it, his screen name is Spanishlover." Romi was enjoying Destiny's reaction.

"Oh, no! You're gonna get raped and mutilated, and I don't have a thing to wear to your funeral!" Destiny was on the floor, rolling around in fake despair.

Romi laughed. "Calm down, Destiny. All he talked about was Texas and music and ideas. He was really fun to talk to. Not like the rest of them who just want to know your shoe size or breast size."

"You didn't tell him, did you?"

"Tell him what?"

"Your shoe size and your breast size!"

"I told you, he didn't ask. The subject never came up."

Destiny was not to be put off so easily. "Don't you *dare* tell him your name, or anything about you, you hear?"

"I hear you. I won't. But he did say that he lived here in Cincinnati."

"That could just be a cover! Did you tell him where you lived?"

"No, of course not."

They got out the second movie and as they put it in the VCR, Destiny was still voicing her concerns about the Internet mystery man. "You know, Romi, those kinds of people can trace you. They have secret codes they put in the computer and then they figure out where your phone line is hooked up and then they come to your house and ring your doorbell and slice your heart out after they have sex with you!"

"Destiny, does your brain ever hurt from all the wild imagining you do?"

"I'm for real, Romi! I didn't make this up. I saw it on TV. You be careful, Romi. Stay away from that guy."

"I'm supposed to talk to him tomorrow after school," Romi said quietly.

"Not a great idea. Anybody with a screen name like Spanishlover is up to no good. I saw a talk show where this one man was giving these girls this drug called Spanish fly. He would drug them, and they wouldn't know if the man was having sex with them or not, and he got them all pregnant."

"Destiny, I think you have sex on your brain. I didn't take any drug from him or have sex with him through the computer screen. I didn't let him know anything about me. All I did was talk to him in a private chat room."

"You went to a private room? I saw another talk show where they used these private chat rooms to bug the phone lines of the people they lured into them. Then they stole their identities and charged up millions of dollars on their credit cards."

"Destiny, you watch too many talk shows! And I don't have a credit card. So I'm safe for now. But I will be careful. I promise."

"Hey, Romi, I have a really serious question for you. This is a deep philosophical question."

"Here we go again. Hit me with it."

"Pizza is round, right?"

"Right."

"And garbage cans are round, right?"

"Right."

"So why are pizza boxes square?"

"Eat your pizza, Destiny."

"Romi?"

"I'm almost afraid to answer."

"The pieces are triangles. Why?"

"Eat your pizza, Destiny. Don't think."

10.

At School

Julio glanced at his watch and darted into the bathroom. He figured he had just enough time to make a pit stop before his last class's bell. He didn't even notice the boy dressed in a purple hooded sweatshirt that hung down to his knees. He was followed by four kids dressed exactly the same. They walked slowly, methodically, forming a tight circle around Julio. A toilet flushed. The boy in the stall, a scrawny kid who looked like he'd been flushed before, took one look at the scene in front of him and ran out of there before he had pulled his pants up completely.

"Hey, Chico!"

Julio tightened his jaw and tensed his fists. "My name's *not* Chico."

"Got something for you, Chico." The boys in purple tightened the circle around Julio.

Julio's fear was turning to anger. "My name is *not* Chico! And you better not get any closer."

They backed away one step, in unison. "Got a message for you. We don't want you here. Got that?"

Julio stepped forward, into the face of the tallest

purple threat. "What do you mean? What did I ever do to you? And who is this 'we' you talking about?"

The tall boy looked coolly into Julio's eyes and showed no fear, only challenge. "You see purple—you get out the way. The Family ain't happy about you being here. We know you from that Texas Tejano gang. You ain't welcome here."

"I don't remember asking you for the welcome wagon! Just stay out of my way or I'll show what Texas Tejano really means!"

"We don't need no wetbacks movin' in here takin' over our territory! We own this area."

"You wouldn't know a wetback if it was dripping on your own yellow back!"

"Watch your mouth, Chico. Or it might get busted."

Julio decided he wasn't going to take any more. "I tell you what," Julio said slowly and clearly. "Why don't *you* stay out of *my* way instead? I don't want to have to tighten you up, but I ain't scared of you, or purple, or The Family. Now move out of my way!"

The figures in the purple circle took one step toward him, stared him down with eyes of hate, then abruptly turned as one and walked out of the bathroom. Julio stood there alone, shaking and angry, in that silent bathroom that smelled of urine and cigarette smoke. They thought he was from one of those Texas gangs he had been running from! Unbelievable! He knew they would only threaten for a while. Then the threats would turn to fists, or knives, or worse. But they wouldn't attack him—not yet. They weren't really sure if he was from that gang, but this was their way of checking him out. They didn't really need a reason to dislike him. They had already decided that.

Julio had started to relax and settle into the new school. His classes were bearable, Ben was a friend who could always make him laugh, and he spent his spare time playing on the computer. A couple of times he had talked to this one girl he thought was from Cincinnati, but who knew. Ben said everybody lied on the Internet. She seemed like somebody he might like to get to know. But he hadn't been able to find her on-line lately. The last time he had talked to her, she said her friend had warned her about Internet perverts, so she didn't feel real comfortable talking to him, then she had signed off quickly.

So now I'm a gang member. And a pervert. Julio sighed as he walked down the hall to class. He was really late, but last bell was band, and he knew Mr. Barnes would understand.

Those gang kids, mused Julio, *separated me right away as different—as Hispanic—as Latino. I wonder what the other kids here see when they see me? I'm tall and thin, but I can take care of myself. I've heard girls giggle behind my back, saying stuff like, "Oh, girl, he is fine!" but nobody's ever told me to my face—yet. My mother thinks I have a nice smile. But mothers are supposed to like you, aren't they?*

Julio walked slowly down the dark, trash-cluttered hallway to class. He did *not* turn around to check for shades of purple behind him.

11.

Phone Calls—
Julio/Diego/Ben

The phone rang, and Julio picked it up as he clicked the thermostat up another notch. He was freezing cold, and the snow outside the window made him shiver with anger as well as the cold.

"*Hola,* my man Julio. How's it going there?" Julio thought his friend's voice sounded particularly far away.

He sighed. "Hey, Diego. Good to hear from you. It snowed all day here. No chance of school being canceled, though. It's just cold and miserable. My feet are still cold, and I gotta get a heavy winter coat or I'm gonna die!"

Diego laughed. "I hate to tell you it's seventy-five today, and I went hang gliding, so I won't. How's the new school?"

"Well, *amigo,* on the very first day of school, before the first class even started, I got into a fight. I mean as soon as I walked in the door, I punched out the face of some kid with green hair."

"You don't play around, do you? You get busted?" Diego asked.

"No, for some reason, the kid covered for me,"

Julio said in amazement. "I didn't see him again all day. I've talked to him since, though. He's OK."

"That's good. What's your classes like? 'Bout like they are here?"

"Yeah, I manage to flounder through them all, keep to myself, and try to be invisible. My English class is reading Walt Whitman, who was pretty radical. History class is stuck at the Civil War. I think all eleventh-grade history classes must be stuck there."

"Yep, we're still on it too. Boring!"

"And guess what? They scheduled me for Spanish One! What a hoot!" laughed Julio.

"That's just plain *estúpido!* Didn't you tell them you were bilingual?"

"Naw, man. Why mess up an easy A? You ought to see the teacher! She's this first-year lady who's from China! Spanish with a Chinese accent! She had me weak!"

"You're gonna go crazy in there, man," Diego sympathized.

"Nah, it gives me something to laugh at, and besides, if I get my schedule changed, I'd have to drop band. The band teacher is cool. Long dreadlocks, a sixties kind of guy. Likes jazz. He was really glad to get a good sax player, and he even asked me to try out for jazz band next week."

"Cool. Meet any girls?"

"Naw, there's no Latina girls here, and I've been too stressed to worry about that kind of stuff. I talked to a girl on the Internet once who seemed really cool, but she thinks I'm some kind of sexual pervert, so I haven't been able to find her again. She was kinda special."

"I'm never too stressed to find women, man. If this little lady turns you on, then keep trying," suggested Diego.

"Yeah, but she might end up being some kind of nine-hundred-pound witch!" Julio exclaimed.

"So what. You're never gonna meet her anyway. The Internet is for pretending, man. Don't worry about reality."

Julio sighed again. "Yeah, I got enough reality here. There's gangs here at this 'super-safe' school that my folks brought me to, seven million miles away from home."

"For real?" Diego seemed astonished.

"Yeah, I almost got jumped in the bathroom already."

"Why you?"

"Why not? I'm new. That's all the reason they need. But you know why they only stared me down and didn't try to punch me out?"

"Your strong right hook on kids with green hair?" Diego laughed.

"Yeah, right. No, they think I belong to a gang from home called the Texas Tejano gang. You ever hear of them?"

"Yeah, man. They're really bad. Guns and a big body count."

"No wonder they just pushed a little. But when they find out I'm not in that gang, and they will, I may have to fight the battle of my life," Julio said with concern.

"Your fist won't stop a bullet, Julio."

"I know. Got any ideas?"

"Join the track team," joked Diego.

"I'm not running away. My parents ran away to bring me here."

"Be careful, Julio," Diego warned him.

"Yeah, man. I will. My other line is ringing. I'll catch you later."

"Peaceout."

Julio clicked the phone to get the other call. "Hello," he said, expecting someone for one of his parents.

"Hey, Julio, what's up, my *amigo* with the strong right hook?" asked Ben's cheerful voice.

Julio smiled. "Hey, Ben, what color is the sky today?"

"The sky is blue and so is my hair. Sky blue. It's my message to spring to hurry up and get here. I'm tired of cold, wet weather."

"What about me? I haven't been warm since I left Texas!"

"I'm starting to lose sympathy for you!" Ben teased.

"Hey, Ben, let me ask you something," Julio said seriously.

"Hit me." Ben was rarely serious.

"What do you know about gangs in the school?"

"I know they're there. Most of the students and all of the teachers pretend that they aren't," Ben replied with derision.

"Yeah, been through that stage before. They close their eyes and think it will go away. That's the way it was at my old school until one of the teachers was killed. Then they started to pay attention, but by that time, it was too late."

"I hear you. It's been getting worse here, though. Fights in the halls, in the bathrooms, at the bus stops. One girl got beat up real bad because she broke up with her boyfriend from The Family," Ben offered.

"I almost got jumped in the bathroom today," admitted Julio.

Ben didn't seem surprised. "Dudes dressed in purple?"

"Yeah."

"Hooded sweatshirts?"

"Yeah."

"You got pushed by the bosses of The Family. They're the strongest at school. Probably about fifty members. Most of them only wear something with purple on it. Only the leaders wear the sweatshirts with hoods."

"The Family," remembered Julio. "Yeah, that's what they called themselves."

"Their real name is the Devildogs. It's supposed to be a secret, but everybody knows it. Were you scared?"

"I was so scared, I coulda peed in my pants, but they didn't know it."

"You watch your back, Julio. These dudes play with real guns," warned Ben.

"Thanks, Ben. I'll be careful."

"Check you out at school tomorrow."

"Later." Julio hung up the phone, feeling both warmed and chilled.

12.

Chat Room 2

Welcome to TEEN TALK, the best partying chat
room on-line! TEEN TALK is open every day,
24 hours a day!
logon//spanishlover
sweetthing: whassup, spanishlover?
spanishlover: sky
cookieman: folks who are high
becool: stars
niobe: nothin's up 'cause I feel down
oogaooga: why you down, baby?
spiceboy: she needs some love
bigmac: let me make your dreams come true
niobe: you ain't my kind of dream. you are
a nightmare!
bigmac: you just wish you could have me.
cookieman: no, she needs sweet dreams
afroqueen: anybody ever have bad dreams?
cookieman: all the time!
becool: I like nightmares. Turns me on!
spiceboy: why?
becool: I'm deep, and I'm weird. I'm going

to write them down one day and make a million dollars.

afroqueen: that's how the story of Frankenstein happened. this lady was on her honeymoon and wrote Frankenstein in her spare time!

niobe: either her new husband was a freak

becool: or he wasn't giving her what she needed!

sweetthing: I have dreams sometimes that I'm dying.

bigmac: now that's freaky!

vanityfair: that's not freaky. everybody has dreams like that sometime.

sweetthing: I heard if you dream you're falling, and you reach the ground, then you really do die.

niobe: nobody has ever proved that

sweetthing: I guess not

niobe: I dreamed once this big black shadow came to get me. I was suffocating. then I woke up with my mom's fur coat on my face.

cookieman: people who wear fur ought to be shot

vanityfair: why? the mink is already dead!

bigmac: I dreamed I got shot once

cookieman: did you die?

bigmac: not yet

afroqueen: I have really scary dreams sometimes

spanishlover: me too

afroqueen: I feel like I'm drowning in the ocean

spanishlover: that must be really scary for someone who can't swim

afroqueen: you making fun of me?

spanishlover: no, I'm trying to sympathize with you

vanityfair: she don't want sympathy

niobe: she needs somebody to read her cards

afroqueen: I got a friend who does that

becool: dreaming about drowning—that's deep

afroqueen: I hear this voice at the end of it. a voice I never heard before.

vanityfair: is it a voice from Heaven?

afroqueen: I don't think so. it's a lover's voice, I think.

vanityfair: a lover? my dreams are never that cool.

spanishlover: I dream about being alone and having no one to talk to

cookieman: I dream about food.

bigmac: go eat something then.

spanishlover: I dream about afroqueen.

sweetthing: ooooooooo!

vanityfair: ooooooooo!

niobe: ooooooooo!

afroqueen: why you dreaming about me?

spanishlover: I don't know. I keep thinking about you.

sweetthing: be careful, afroqueen.

niobe: beware of perverts and weirdos.

afroqueen: make it clear, spanishlover
spanishlover: I'm no pervert. I enjoyed our private chat. that's all.
vanityfair: watch out!
niobe: check him out, afroqueen. we got your back!
bigmac: yeah, give him ten minutes in a chat room. let him talk.
afroqueen: spanishlover, you want to go to a chat room?
becool: be cool, you two
spanishlover: please
afroqueen: OK. See you there.

Dear Afroqueen:
Thanks for coming in here to talk to me. It sounds like we really went to a room or something. We're floating someplace in cyberspace. The only difference is that the rest of them can't see what we're writing.

Spanishlover:
I had lots of people warn me about on-line predators. You hear on the news about stupid girls who run away with some old man after he talks to them in the chat rooms. Now I certainly don't consider myself to be stupid, but I have sense enough to be careful.

Let me see if I can ease your fears. I don't know enough to be a pervert. I'm sixteen years old, and in the eleventh grade, and I just moved to Ohio from Texas. I checked in a few weeks ago to Thomas Jefferson High School in Cincinnati, and the only kid I know really well is Ben Olsen, who has blue or green or red or purple hair.

Well, shut me up! That's the school I go to! Did you get in a fight with Ben on the first day of school?

That was me! But don't think I'm some kind of troublemaker. It had been a really bad morning, and Ben's nose got introduced to my fist before I met the rest of him. I think he's a pretty cool dude.

I heard about that, and I know Ben. I think I may have even seen you in the hall. You're always by yourself.

I told you I have this dream, this fear of being alone.

So why don't you make friends?

It's hard being the new kid in the middle of the year. It's even harder when you're different.

What do you mean different? You got two heads or something?

No, I mean, there's lots of Anglo kids at our school. And lots of black kids. But I'm probably the only Hispanic kid in the whole school.

Does that bother you?

A little. Probably more than a little. At my old school, it was about eighty percent Hispanic.

I feel you. I'd hate to have to move to another city and state. I've known most of the kids here since elementary school.

Yeah, that's the way it was at my old school too. My friend Diego and I went to kindergarten together.

That's rough. But most of the kids at Jefferson are pretty friendly. Give us a chance. You gotta reach out.

Not all of them are friendly. And some have already reached out and almost touched me. You ever heard of The Family?

The Devildogs? They been sweatin' you?

Yeah, real sweat. They don't like the fact I'm new or that I'm Hispanic.

What did they do?

Just threatened me in the bathroom, but I know what they can do if they want to. I came here partly because of the gangs at home.

Well, those of us who don't do gangs will watch your back. Hey, when's your lunch bell?

I have first lunch.

Me too. I hate that. It's so early in the morning, I'm never very hungry. You want to meet at lunch tomorrow? Maybe I can introduce you to my friends.

Bet! And I won't wear anything purple!

Good idea. What do you look like?

I'll be the tall, good-looking guy with the bottle of hot sauce in his hand. I'll meet you at that table in the back near the pop machine.

Hey, I don't even know your name.

Julio. Julio Montague. And you, my African Queen, what's your name?

My name is Romiette Cappelle. I'll be wearing an orange sweater and a big smile. (I'll probably have on shoes and jeans too—didn't want you to get the wrong idea!) You're the new guy—it will be easy to spot you. See you soon.

Peaceout.

13.

Romiette's Journal

So they were all wrong. He wasn't a psychopath or a pervert. He was just a dude, a **really** good-looking one—wow—who needed somebody to be a friend. Today I had lunch with Julio. Destiny and I have the same lunch bell, so we usually see each other at lunch. But she was absent today with a cold, so I headed to the lunchroom alone. I just wasn't prepared for what happened. When I first saw him, I sucked in my breath and forgot to exhale. He looked so much better than any of the boys around here. He has really dreamy eyes, but of course, who notices such things? I've never really paid much attention to what boys look like. But Julio was different. He was funny and friendly and so easy to talk to. And so easy to look at!

He was standing there, up on top of the table, dressed in a jeans jacket and a Texas Rangers T-shirt, holding a bottle of hot sauce in one hand and a red rose in the other. He seemed to know exactly who I was, because he jumped off the table just as I approached and bowed low and handed me the rose. He said he brought the rose because the hot sauce was too great a treasure and he couldn't give it up. We talked about school (he hates it—at least here), cold weather (he hates it), snow (he hates it), and Texas (he loves it).

We hit it off so good. We talked so much and laughed so hard that we forgot to eat lunch. The bell rang, and we both looked up and realized that we hadn't taken one bite out of our food, and lunch was already over. We laughed and promised to meet again for lunch tomorrow. I can't wait to talk to him again. He's not like any guy I ever met. He's witty, and wise, and oh my goodness—he's cute too. I've got to get my homework done in a hurry—we've got a one-on-one session scheduled on the computer at nine tonight. I can't believe this—I can't wait. What is happening to me? I gotta call Destiny!

14.

Phone Call

Just as Romi picked up the phone to call Destiny, it rang. "Hey, Destiny," Romi greeted her. "I was just getting ready to call you."

"Well, Romi, you know I've been working on developing my psychic abilities. With you, it's easy. Something happened today. Tell me!"

Romi was never really sure if Destiny was just lucky, or if she really did have some extrasensory abilities. "How did you know?" she asked in amazement.

"When will you learn to appreciate my psychic powers?" Destiny replied. "Spill it, girl."

"I met the dude from the Internet," Romi began. "I had lunch with him," she added, just to agitate Destiny even more.

"You what? Are you crazy? Where? When?"

"At school." Romi was enjoying this—making Destiny crazy with questions.

"You met a grown man at school? Have you lost your mind?"

"I thought you were psychic," teased Romi.

"I am, but you're messing up the interstellar vibes."

"He's no grown man. He's the same age as we are."

"A sixteen-year-old is a sexual stalker?" Destiny was totally confused.

Romi laughed out loud. "I keep telling you. He's not a stalker or a pervert. He's the new kid—the one who transferred here from Texas a few weeks ago."

"The one who dyed Ben's nose to match his hair?"

"Yeah, that's the one. And he didn't mean to hit Ben."

"He's the one you've been talking to?"

"Yeah, and all the time he was going to school right here."

"Talk about psychic," Destiny said in admiration. "You got the stars with you, girl. This is too freaky. What's his sign?"

"I don't know. I didn't ask."

Destiny screamed into the phone, "How many times do I have to tell you. That's the *first* thing you ask. How are you gonna know if you're compatible or not?"

"We just talked," Romi replied, unconcerned. "That seemed compatible enough. He's fun to talk to. And Destiny, he is so fine!"

"I hear you, girl. And I have not heard this from you before. He's gotta be an Aries or a Sagittarius— those are the fire signs. Since you are a Leo, you know that's your best bet unless you want to go with your opposite, which is an Aquarius—something I would not advise! Fire and water do not mix, girlfriend."

"You're nuts, Destiny. He could be an Aquarius. I don't know."

"How can you have lunch with a dude and not be sure of his sign?"

"I'll find out for you, OK? Relax. All I did was eat lunch with him one day. We didn't make wedding plans." Romi laughed.

"I sure hope his sign is compatible—this may be your soul mate."

"Don't get carried away, Destiny," warned Romi. "I'm not sure if I believe in all that stuff you do about soul mates. All I know is . . . he's really . . . really . . . I can't put my finger on it, but he makes me feel special."

"Uh-oh! The special finger feeling. I sure hope that Scientific Soul Mate System package arrives soon. Looks like we're gonna need it!"

"Maybe not . . . ," mused Romi.

"Girl, I may have to get my cards out for you. You're movin' into serious territory awfully quick. You eating with him again tomorrow?"

"I think so. I hope so." Romi could feel herself blushing.

"Oh, no—now she's hoping! I hate that I have to make up that test at lunch tomorrow. Meet me at my locker after school. And find out his birthday!"

"For sure, I will," Romi promised. "Hey, Destiny?" she added.

"What it is?"

"Do you realize that when we've been talking about incompatibility and stuff, we've only been talking about sun signs?"

"Yeah, so what's your point?"

"He's Hispanic."

"So?"

"And I'm black."

"So?"

"Neither one of us noticed."

"Good, that's the way the world ought to be." Destiny had her own sense of world order.

"Yeah, you're right," agreed Romi. "I'll wait for you after last bell tomorrow."

"OK. Later, girl."

Romi hung up the phone, thinking about what Destiny had said.

15.

Julio and Ben

Julio bounded into the band room, jumped over a music stand, and grabbed a bass viol and started to dance. Mr. Barnes, the teacher with the dreadlocks, just grinned. Ben, who was on the floor under the snare drum looking for his drumsticks, glanced at Julio with amusement.

"So who put ants in your pants and made you want to dance, *Señor* Julio?" Ben asked as he slid from under the drum. His hair was bright orange today.

"Hey, Ben, my orange-haired *amigo!* Today I had lunch with a girl that at my old school, I never would have even noticed, but yes, I would have had to notice her. She's so pretty. She's brown, golden-crispy . . . like . . . like . . . I sound like I'm describing fried chicken, and that's not fair at all."

"Who is this foxy babe?"

"Her name is Romiette Cappelle. She is the prettiest girl I've ever met. That orange sweater made her brown skin and hazel eyes seem to glow.

Or maybe it was her smile. When she smiled, she was like sunshine or something."

"Yeah, I know Romi. She's cool. But I've never seen her shine like that. Sounds like you're the one who was glowing!"

"Why is this coming out all wrong? I can't find the words to describe how I feel. I feel stupid and silly."

The rest of the class straggled into the room, and the bell rang. Everybody ignored it, however, including the teacher, who was helping students get their instruments tuned or tightened. Julio took out his saxophone and rubbed a soft cloth over it lovingly. He wasn't thinking about music, though. His mind was at lunch.

Ben added, "I've known Romiette since seventh grade. She is a class act. Smart. Pretty. And proud."

Julio mused, "You know what, Ben? I stood on a chair in front of the whole cafeteria and handed her a rose. I didn't care who saw me, or what they thought. I would have tap-danced on the table in a bowl of mashed potatoes if she had asked me to."

"You got it bad, Julio. Dancing in mashed potatoes?"

"All I know is she is the funniest, smartest, prettiest girl I've ever talked to. She made me laugh with her descriptions of her father on TV and his unbelievable news partner. I've got to watch the six o'clock news tonight."

"Oh, yeah, good old Nannette. The whole town

watches the news just to watch her mess up."

"And Romiette seemed really interested in my stories about my old school, and all my lies about Texas."

"You lied? I'm proud of you, Julio. You're such a quick learner."

"Naw, man. We just talked about stupid stuff—like teachers and homework. We talked as if we had known each other forever. She likes music and sports and books."

"Does this perfect woman have any faults?"

"One weakness—she can't swim—but that's OK, I can teach her! Listen to me—I'm thinking about teaching a girl I just met how to swim."

"This is something really new for you, I guess."

"Oh, *sí!* She's not like any girl I ever met before. She's got class and style and a kind of spark. The girls back home just didn't have it. She makes me feel comfortable and relaxed and natural. We're going to talk tonight at nine on-line after we do our homework. I can't believe this. For the first time since I moved here, I feel alive!"

"I'm glad for you, man. Go for it!"

The band teacher tossed his dreads, rapped on the podium, and started warm-ups. Band class was the last bell of the day, and they were all tired, so he tried to make it upbeat and fun. He grinned at Julio, as if they shared a secret, and led the group to a march beat. Julio, excited yet relaxed, grinned back and played like he was Kenny G.

16.

Computer Chat

Dear Romiette:
Meeting you and talking to you was the high
point of my day. You can make a cold day
sizzle and a gray afternoon burn bright
red. I know that you know everybody at that
school, and that you're really popular. It
was nice of you to spend time with a new
kid.
Julio

Julio:
If you think the only reason I ate lunch with
you (we never did get around to eating, did we?)
was because you were the new kid and I felt
sorry for you, you're dumber than I thought you
were. And quiet as it's kept, I'm not Miss
Popularity. Sure, I have friends, but I'm no
showstopper. I sat with you today because I
wanted to. I've never met anybody like you
before. You were so much fun to be with and to
talk to. It must be the Texas hot sauce, because

nobody around here even comes close to you in how you make me feel. I guess I shouldn't say that, or admit that you make me feel different from any other boy I've ever met, but I don't feel up to being shy and playing those boy-girl games. Or maybe it's because we're not exactly face-to-face and I can write what I'm feeling easier than I can say it.

Romiette:
I know exactly what you mean. All day I've been thinking of you. I feel like I've known you forever and I want to know you forever more. When I'm old and wrinkled and eighty, I want to be able to talk to you. Does that sound stupid? I'm not afraid to tell you that I like you. Tomorrow when I see you, I have a surprise for you.

I love surprises. Just no hot sauce, OK? And call me Romi.

Romi. What a nice nickname. No hot sauce. I guarantee you'll like the surprise. Tell me, if you could win a million-dollar lottery, what would you do?

I wouldn't do anything stupid like buy a million new outfits, I know that. Maybe just a thousand. Seriously, I don't know. I'm pretty happy with my life as it is—my friends and family, the sunshine, and my golden retrievers. Our dog just had puppies a few weeks ago. Want one?

I'm like you. There's lots more that I think is important besides money. Puppies for one. I would love to have a golden retriever puppy. If my mom will let me. I'll ask—but I'm sure she will. She knew how much I hated leaving my dog behind, but she was a German shepherd and she was old, so we left her at my grandpa's ranch, where she had lots of kids to play with and lots of space.

I hope you can have one of the puppies. Now you answer this one for me. If you had to die by fire or by water, which would you choose?

If I had to die—and I don't plan to any-time soon—I guess I'd choose to die by water. Fire hurts. Water is cool and soothing and at least will comfort you before you get swallowed up in it. Why do you ask?

No real reason. I think you can learn a lot about a person by their answer. Me, I'm scared of water, so I guess I'd choose fire. But you're right—fire hurts. Maybe I'll just die in bed when I'm ninety-nine. Hey, when is your birthday?

March third. Why?

My friend Destiny is into astrology. March third—that makes you a Pisces, right?

Does that mean anything?

Destiny will know. She won't even look at a boy unless he's the right sign.

So what sign are you?

I'm a Leo: bright, sunny, cheerful—also regal and dominating, if you want to know the rest.

Lions are my favorite pets! I can handle it! See you tomorrow. Gotta go—bye!

Peaceout. Bye for now.

17.

Conversation

Julio turned off his computer and smiled. For the first time since he had moved from Texas, he looked around his small room with contentment. His room back in Corpus Christi was huge with a large window that he liked to open at night to let in the fresh evening breezes. This room barely had space enough to turn around in, but his bed and desk and other furniture fit neatly into each corner. The walls were freshly painted, but bare. So Julio dragged one of the unopened boxes out of the closet on which his mother had neatly written Julio's room. He opened it slowly, trying not to remember the feeling of loss and anger that he had felt when he packed away the life he knew.

Rolled on the top were his posters. The first one he tacked to the wall next to his bed was a purple-toned photo of Louis Armstrong playing his trumpet. He always liked that poster because it seemed to Julio that Louis Armstrong really enjoyed playing his horn, that he was happy just to be making music. The other poster was of a sailboat on a lake. The sky was bright with sunshine and promise, the boat dipped with confidence on the deep blue lake, and the sailor, a small figure on the deck, grinned with confidence that same smile of satisfaction and peace.

Near the bottom of the box were other items that Julio no longer needed but refused to give up yet, reminders of his childhood.

—A baseball card of Hank Aaron. Probably not worth much since it had been ripped and taped together. That fight with Diego when they were seven was not over the card, but over the bubble gum inside. It was much later they realized the value of the card, but it was too late.

—His rock collection. His fifth-grade teacher had made the class collect one of each kind of rock or stone. Julio had searched for weeks, finally finding just about all of them. Igneous rocks, sandstone, granite. He loved the cool smoothness of them, their quiet strength. Everybody else had tossed or lost their rock collection. Julio kept them in a small plastic box. He knew the name of each one.

—His books. The one he read for a book report last year in school that he was sure he would hate, but ended up loving. His book on music. A book he had read from cover to cover several times about television and film making. A dictionary. A computer manual. He set those on his desk.

—His video games. He hadn't set the machine up yet because he had no TV in his room here. Back home, he had never been upset when his mother sent him to his room because he had a TV, a stereo, a video game player, and a phone. She finally figured it out and after that sent him in the backyard to cut the grass or clean the gutters when she wanted to punish him.

—He had unpacked his CDs on the first day. He couldn't live without music. But in the box were tapes that he had liked a couple of years ago. He got those out and tossed them in his desk drawer.

—A small stuffed lion. He plumped it up and looked it over. He had won it tossing baseballs at the state fair last year. It looked at him with a silly grin. He could never explain why he had kept it, but now he was glad. *Romiette will love it,* he thought.

Just then his father knocked on his door.
"Hi, Papa. Where's Mom?"
"She went to the grocery store. How was school today?" Luis Montague was a tall man, with broad

shoulders, a huge mustache, and slightly graying hair. He had served in Vietnam for a year, then finished college and started in the insurance business. He looked at his son with pride. Julio would one day look just like his father, but he carried his mother's spark and sensibility. Julio would choose to fight when confronted with a problem, where his father would try to talk his way out of it. Luis admired that, but he often feared his son's leaps would lead him into trouble.

"It was better, Papa. Much better." Julio couldn't tell his father why, at least not yet.

"Good. Are your classes difficult?" Luis asked with interest.

"Not really. I like band."

Luis grinned. "Of that I have no doubt, but what about the academics?"

"No sweat, Papa. I'll be able to handle it. It's just hard coming here in the middle of the school year."

"I know, Julio. I understand how rough this is. Are you making any friends?"

"Well, I met a really nice girl."

"A girl? Now that's a good sign that things might be looking up. Is she pretty?"

"Yeah, Papa, she's really fine. She's smart and funny and she makes me smile. I like talking to her. We met on the Internet. It's funny—I was on a chat line in a room with a bunch of people, and she was in the room too, and I said something about hating it here and missing Texas. Somehow she stood out in that crowded room. It turned out she lives here in

Cincinnati, and before we knew it, we were in a private chat room, zipping messages back and forth." Julio's face was animated and excited just talking about Romiette.

"You spend too much time on that computer."

The smile on Julio's face dimmed. He grew sullen and much quieter. "You want me to have friends, don't you?"

"Yes, son, but *real* people, not voices on a computer screen. You need to get out in the world more." Luis just couldn't understand Julio's fascination with the chat rooms. Computers were for calculations or file gathering—for work. Chat rooms were a waste of time, as far as Luis could tell.

"That's what I've been trying to tell you, Papa! You don't ever listen to me! This girl I met on the Internet is a real person. She goes to my school. And I like her! Is that real enough for you?"

"I'm sorry, Julio. I'm glad you've found someone to take away the loneliness."

"Papa, she has some golden retriever puppies. She's giving them away. Do you think maybe . . . since I had to leave King . . ."

"Perhaps. Ask your mother. Our place here is so small. What is this girl's name? You brighten up when you speak of her. She must have made quite an impression in so short a time."

"Yeah, she did. Her name is Romiette."

"Is she . . . ah . . . French?"

"No, Papa. She's black."

"Black?"

"Black. African-American. Black."

"Oh. Uh, is that . . . wise?"

"Wise? What do you mean?" Julio felt his jaws begin to tighten.

His father sat down on the bed and sighed. "Well," he said slowly, "we hear so many terrible things on the news, and you know what problems we had back in Corpus Christi with the black gangs, and it seems like we just escaped from all those problems, and now, the first person you hook up with is some black kid."

Julio's anger erupted. "She's not just 'some black kid'! She's smart and nice, and she's one of the few people in that whole school who's been friendly to me since I've been there. Have you forgotten that gangs of Mexican kids roamed our school and were fighting with the black kids back home? And on the news at home, who were the bad guys, Papa?"

Julio's eyes were challenging and fiery. His father decided not to push the fight. "You're right, son. I'm sorry. I overreacted. It's not as if you're going to marry this girl. I'm glad you've found a friend. And sure, let's get a puppy. Perhaps it will make this place feel like home." But his father sighed once more as he left Julio's room, as if he sensed trouble ahead.

18.

Romiette's Journal

I met Julio at lunch yesterday again. He wasn't standing on the table this time, but he was there before I was. He grinned and looked really glad to see me, and suddenly, I felt shy. I wondered if my hair was smooth, or my breath was smelly, or my shirt was wrinkled. But as soon as we started talking, I forgot all that. His voice has a soft lilt to it that makes me feel comfortable and safe. He told me all about his home in Texas, and his grandfather's ranch, and his friends there.

I found myself wondering if he had a girl back in Texas. Surely someone as good-looking as Julio would have a girlfriend. But he never mentioned it, and I didn't have the nerve to ask. I wonder why I even care. He's just a guy at school, but he's so much more than that. I look forward to seeing him, talking to him, being with him. I think about him when we're not together and wonder what he's doing. This is not like me, and I don't even mind.

All through my morning classes I found myself

thinking about that stupid surprise he talked about. When I got to lunch, I found on the table a small stuffed lion. It was furry and soft and the color of caramel pudding. I looked at him hesitantly and smiled.

"For you," he said simply. "Keep it close to you, and think of me when you touch it." He looked suddenly embarrassed and pretended to be fixing the bright orange bow around the neck of the little lion. I'd never been given a gift that was so thoughtful and wonderful. I felt all shy and embarrassed again, like my thoughts were naked or something.

"I love it," I said quietly, hugging the little lion close to me. "I'm going to call him Pudding."

He said, "Keep him in your book bag, and when you reach in to get a notebook, or lunch money, or a peppermint, I'll be there with you." How did he manage to make a stupid piece of golden fuzz seem like a million-carat diamond?

I wanted to give him something then—something to show I was interested, but not too personal. I dug down in my book bag and came up with my little gold key chain. It had my initials—RRC—engraved on it. I got it for my birthday last year. I wanted him to have it. I told him as I gave it to him, "Hang on to this until I get some car keys, OK?" He rubbed it shiny with the tail of his T-shirt, hooked it onto a loop of his jeans, and said he'd be glad to be "the keeper of my keys." Somehow he made that sound sexy.

We sat there grinning at each other, ignoring the rest of the cafeteria, the rest of the school, the rest of the world. Then the trouble started. Halfway through lunch Rashad and Terrell, two dudes who hang with the gangbangers, stopped by our table. I remember both of them from kindergarten—they used to be silly and sweet, but they scare me now. It's like they're angry all the time. They walk around the halls with matching purple jackets and frowns. They never do homework, but even the teachers seem a little scared and don't bother them about it. I'm not sure if they're in the gang, because nobody comes out and says so, especially to somebody like me, but they all hang together on the corner by the bus stop after school. They take kids' bus money and sometimes even push kids around or knock them down.

Anyway, they stopped at our table and just stared at us. They didn't say anything. They just looked. Julio glanced at them, started to say something, but changed his mind and decided to ignore them. They left after a few minutes, but they looked real hard at me, as if to give me some unspoken message. They left a chill behind them.

The silly, friendly mood of our lunch conversation had been ruined. We finished quickly and promised to write tonight on E-mail. Neither one of us said much. It's hard to know what to be afraid of when you don't even know what the threat is.

19.

Julio and Ben

The final bell rang. All the band equipment was put away, and Julio and Ben headed out to catch their bus. Julio stopped by his locker to get his history book, and Ben, hair buttercup yellow today, put his history book away.

"Don't you ever do homework, Ben?" Julio asked as he tossed his book into his bag.

"Not if I can help it, man. Homework goes against everything I believe in, like freedom and independence. How am I going to start a revolution like Sam Adams and his boys did back in 1776 if I don't practice now?"

"But you get good grades anyway," Julio noted in admiration.

"Ah, my friend who needs his nose pierced, I read all the time—much more than the teacher assigns. I go to the library and I get so involved with the stories and the lives of the people in the history book that I end up knowing enough to teach the class. But I'd never tell the teacher. He thinks I'm Ben the weirdo. That's cool with me."

"You've got enough body piercing for both of us. Is that a new one on your eyebrow?"

"Yeah, I was bored, and it drives my mother crazy. You know, I'll probably end up being the corporate lawyer she wants me to be, but I'm gonna have fun on the journey!"

"Like the safety pins in your ears?"

"Why buy jewelry? I believe in self-expression."

"For real. I bet little old ladies on the bus get up and move when they see you coming."

"Yeah, I love it! Here I come—leather jacket, dog collar on my neck, blue or pink or green hair, and all my visible body parts pierced. I sit down next to one of them, and look real slowly over at her, and then I grin—showing lots of teeth."

"Why you do that, man?" Julio asked, laughing.

"Why not? Life's a trip—enjoy the ride. So, speaking of trippin', how was dining with Miss Dynamite today, *mi amigo?*

Julio grinned at the thought of Romiette, then frowned as he remembered the rest. "Lunch today with Romi was great, at least at first. We laughed and rattled on together like we've known each other for years. We talked about her mom's shop and her dad's TV show. That Nannette Norris is a real trip."

"Yeah, I saw it last night! She kept stumbling over words like 'maintenance' and 'metropolitan.' It would have been funny if it weren't so embarrassing. Old Nannette is my kind of girl! Pretty—and stupid!"

Julio added, "It looks like Romi's dad tries real hard to keep a straight face, but in those little sections just before the commercials when they have to make small talk on the air, you can see he's straining to act like he likes her. It must be rough."

Ben and Julio walked down to the corner, past the little store where kids bought chips and soda and illegal cigarettes. The weather was cold, but the sun was shining, letting them know spring would show up sooner or later. They had missed the early bus, so they knew they had at least a twenty-minute wait. They stood in silence for a few minutes, Ben's corn-bright hair blowing in the chilly breeze. Ben said finally, "So, tell me, did you give Romi the lion?"

Julio laughed. "Yeah, I was scared at first, but I think she liked my little surprise. And even though it was just a small stuffed lion, she treated it like it was a gift from a king!"

Ben bowed down in mock reverence and announced, "All hail, King Julio!"

Julio punched his arm, chuckling. "Cut that out, Ben!"

"Oh, sire, tell me. Did the Princess Romiette honor you with a gift as well, or have you changed your initials to RRC and decided to advertise it on the loop of your jeans?" He wouldn't stop bowing. Other students at the bus stop smiled, but they were used to Ben's antics.

"Yeah, she gave me the key chain," he admitted.

"Aw. How sweet." He was still bowing, only

now he looked more like a penguin than the subject of a king.

"I wasn't sure if I should take it at first," Julio began.

"Why?" Ben finally stood straight up. "You think too much, man!"

"But it seemed like she really wanted me to have it, so I thanked her and hooked it onto my own key chain, this one with the Texas Rangers logo on it."

"Good man. Wise choice. So, a perfect day?"

"Not exactly. The Family is still in the house."

"This ain't good, Julio."

"You telling me? Me and Romi were just finishing the last of the cafeteria chocolate milk, which is probably the only thing they can't mess up, and these two dudes came up to our table and stopped. I looked up to say something, thinking they were friends of Romiette's, but they didn't smile. And they had on purple."

"What did you do?"

"There was nothing to do. They just stared at me. I don't think they liked me talking to her. They didn't say anything; they just looked at me, looked at her, and walked away."

"What you gonna do?"

"Wait and see. And watch my back—for now."

"What does Romi think?"

"I don't know. I thought I had escaped that stuff. She looked as scared as I was. I think she knew them, but they weren't friends of hers. Why should anybody care who I have lunch with? Romiette is the only girl in the whole school who's been friendly to me, and now we're threatened because of it?"

"What did she say?"

"We didn't talk about it after they left. We both left the cafeteria in a hurry. We promised to write each other on E-mail, but I wonder what she thinks about all this. I wonder if this will spoil something that hasn't even had a chance to start yet. And I wonder if she's as scared as I am."

"Don't let the Purple Panthers sweat you, man. Maybe they're just showin' off."

"I don't think so. They'll be back—I'm sure of it."

"Just chill, and ignore them. You coming to jazz band tryouts next week? You're pretty good on the saxophone."

"And you're not bad on the drums!" Julio returned.

"Percussion is my life!" howled Ben as he pounded on his book bag like a drum. "I just love to make noise!"

"Do you play other instruments?" Julio asked. The bus, finally, could be seen in the distance lumbering slowly toward them.

Ben shrugged. "Clarinet, vibes, bongos. And I'm a drummer in a rock band on weekends. What can I say—I'm a musician extraordinaire, *Señor* Julio! You play anything else besides that sax?"

"I can play the mandolin," Julio admitted

sheepishly. "Not much use for that in a marching band."

"For real? You got one?"

"Yeah, I brought it with me from Texas."

"That's phat. How good are you?"

"Whenever you have an opening in your rock band for an extra mandolin payer, I'm your man, Ben! Actually, I'm pretty good. I played a little on weekends with a small Tejano band in Corpus Christi. I miss all that stuff."

"It must be rough moving so far from home. I've lived here all my life. Maybe that's why I try to liven things up around here. Everything's the same, especially in the winter—kinda . . ."

"Gray!"

"You got it. So I wear yellow hair and safety pins and nobody knows all I want to do is make music."

"You're OK, Ben. I'll bring my mandolin one day and show you how to play it."

"Don't worry about me—that's the kind of thing that melts a girl's socks off. Somebody like Romiette would think it was sooo romantic!"

"You make good sense even if you do have a ring in your nose!"

"It only hurts when I sneeze."

"Or when somebody knocks it off your face!"

"Don't remind me. Here's my bus. Catch you tomorrow!"

"Later, man. Here's my bus pulling up in the rear."

20.

At the Boutique

Romiette sometimes complained to her friends, but she loved working at her mother's store. She'd take the short bus ride from school to the shop, and always, just before she went inside, she'd stand a few yards from the door and watch the people who passed by, those who looked, and those who went inside. Downtown sidewalks were always busy with shoppers, commuters, and the thousands of nameless people who worked in the offices. Romi called them "the suits" and "the shoes." "The suits" were the men in the office uniform—dark jacket, dark slacks (khaki on Friday), reddish tie, white shirt. They all carried briefcases and all of them believed themselves to be much more important than they really were. The really important ones didn't have to walk where they needed to go. Someone drove them. "The shoes" were the women who wore variations of the men's uniform, only they wore huge, white athletic shoes with their blue suits. They carried their stylish shoes in a bag, and walked purposefully in their play shoes to their destination, where they did not play. They were serious and focused, these women, determined to make it in a man-made world. Romi admired them.

People who usually had no time to notice whether the weather had changed, or the homeless person sitting on the corner, would often slow down at the window of the boutique. Lady Brianna Cappelle had a sense of style and drama, and her window displays were delightfully eye-catching. This month the display included three stained-glass windows crafted with intricate flower designs, a fountain from which bubbled clear, cool water, dozens of live tulips blooming two months early, and a sampling of outfits placed artfully among them. Sometimes people just walked in out of curiosity. Most of them left with a purchase or two.

Every time Romi walked into the store, she would stop to enjoy the sensory feast inside. Fountains bubbled, soft music soothed, and mild incense, blended with the smell of new cloth and old stories, made Romi grin with delight. It was here that she learned of all the African tribes—those of the past who established great kingdoms long before European kingdoms began, and those of the present who lived and worked with great dignity and pride. It was here that Romi had heard the wondrous folktales of the storytellers, and it was here that Romi and her mother had become very close. They worked well together, and as Romi got older she had been given more responsibility. She liked being in the store alone too, as she was today. Her mother had run to the bank for a few minutes, and Romi decided to rearrange the jewelry display since the store was practically empty. The door chimed as it opened, and Malaka Grimes walked in.

Romi and Malaka had been friends when they were much younger and lived near each other. But Malaka's parents had divorced, Malaka had moved, and she had grown up facing lots of pain and unhappiness. It had changed her from the giggly, cheerful friend Romi remembered to a hard-acting, foulmouthed girl who smoked, drank, and wore her skirts very tight and very short. When they ran into each other at school last year, Romi almost didn't recognize Malaka. They had exchanged phone numbers, promised to call, but there was very little to say anymore.

"Whassup, Romiette," Malaka said coolly. She was wearing a body-hugging purple sweater, a short black leather skirt, and purple tights.

"Hey, girl. Not much. Just chillin' here in my mom's store."

"Got any new stuff in?" Malaka fingered the jewelry, then tossed it back onto the counter as if it were junk.

"Yeah, some live Kente cloth dresses over there, and some jewelry to die for in that case over there." Romi felt uncomfortable. Malaka had not come to shop.

"Doesn't your mama give you whatever you want out of here?" Malaka asked.

"Give? You must be crazy! My mother is in

business for the money. She pays me for workin', so she expects me to pay for things I see and like. She takes it out of my check."

"From what I've seen you wear, you must not get a very big check." Malaka laughed sarcastically.

"Yeah, I had to learn to control myself." Romi busied herself by dusting the jewelry case. She was trying not to treat Malaka with suspicion, but she couldn't figure out what she wanted.

Finally Malaka let her purpose be known. "Hey, Romi," she said innocently, "who was that I saw you eatin' lunch with?"

Romi knew instantly where the conversation was headed. This she could handle. She paused a minute, looked Malaka up and down slowly, adjusted the water flow from the fountain, then turned to Malaka and said boldly, "That new boy, Julio. What's it to you?"

"The Puerto Rican?"

"He's not Puerto Rican, he's Mexican. Actually, he's Texan. He's from Corpus Christi."

"He's kinda cute, if you like that type." Malaka sauntered past Romi as if to look at the candle display.

"What do you mean, 'that type'?" Romi could feel the anger building.

"Well, you know, Mexican—Hispanic-like."

"What's wrong with that?" Romi felt as if she needed to defend Julio. She wasn't sure why, but she felt protective.

"Nothin'. Hey, why you gettin' all salty? I just said—" Malaka was enjoying this. She knew she was irritating Romi. That was her purpose.

"You acted like something was wrong with me eating lunch with a Mexican-American."

"I don't see why you would want to—you know, you've always been heavy into African clothes and jewelry and stuff. It just seemed odd to see you giggling like a third grader with that kid that's so obviously—let me see how I can put this—Spanish." Malaka smirked.

"I was *not* giggling. He's funny and clever and he makes me laugh. What's it to you, anyway?"

"Ain't nothin' to me. Some other folks, now—they might give a care. Do what you want. Can't even have a conversation with you no more. Catch you later. Peace." At that, Malaka sauntered out of the store.

Romi stood there shaking and angry. "Peace? Doesn't look like it. I wonder what that was all about. Something's going on here."

21.
Phone Call

Romi lounged on her bed and waited for the phone to ring. She'd finished her homework, taken her shower, talked to Destiny twice, and now, just before sleep took over, she knew that Julio would call. She picked it up on the second ring. *No use letting him think I'm desperate!* she thought.

"*Hola,* Romi." Julio's voice melted her socks, but she wasn't going to let him know, at least not yet.

"What's up, Julio? You dealin' with that purple warning we got today?"

"So what was that all about? I could tell you knew those thick-lookin' dudes, but they didn't seem like they wanted to sit down and share a Coke and a smile."

Romi sighed. "Julio, we got gangbangers like everybody else. They just never bothered me before."

"I know. I can smell gangbangers from a distance, and those dudes were stinking with their power and threat. They've been hassling me, but you've got nothing to do with that."

"Hassling you? Why?"

"Because they can. At my old school, it got so bad that they'd walk into a hall and everyone would run inside the nearest classroom. Teachers too. One teacher, Mr. Cordero, tried to stand up to them last year. He insisted they take off their colors in his class and he refused to run the other way when they 'walked the hall,' as they called it. He would look them straight in the eye and tell them he was not afraid of them. He died in a car accident one weekend. His brakes failed. So they say. No one could prove anything, but the gangbangers walked the halls with more freedom after that. The principal, a timid little man, wrote letters and sent memos, but he would lock his office doors when it was time for 'gang walk.'"

"Oh, Julio. That's scary. Did you have a lot of gangs?"

"We had some. There was an all-girl gang who called themselves the Sisterhood—really just a bunch of little wanna-bes who wanted to be bad, and wanted to be noticed, and wanted to be seen with the dudes in the main gangs. The big gangs had organized crime connections from New York. I know because the gangs seemed to show up all of a sudden. We had about five new kids enroll in the school—hard-looking dudes who didn't look like eleventh graders. They spent a lot of time hanging with the 'fringe' kids—you know, the kids who come late or skip school or hang on the corners after midnight. Before we knew it, there were meetings, and colors, and handshakes, and all of a sudden those kids had money and drugs and clothes and . . . power, I guess is the best way to say it. And those five transfer kids dropped out—just left. Our school was rough before, but it changed. Instead of fistfights, kids got cut with knives. I knew lots of kids who had guns in their book bags."

"Guns in their book bags? But I guess I shouldn't be surprised. I know the same kinds of kids. I bet they look the same. Not much nerve. No real friends. Scary. Like on the news. You got racial gangs? Or mixed, like in *West Side Story*?"

"Yeah, I remember *West Side Story*. Our English teacher showed it to us last year when we read *Romeo and Juliet*. That was a good movie. I remember one gang was 'Americans'—mostly white kids, but I think they threw a couple of black kids in there to make it look good. The other gang was Puerto Rican kids. Their leader was played by an actor who was Greek. So much for Hollywood."

"Reality is a lot scarier."

"You got that right. Romi, did you notice that our names are almost like the ones in the play, only backwards? Do you think that means something? Are we destined for doom or romance? Or is it just weird?"

Romi grinned, glad that Julio had noticed too. "Yeah, I recognized our names. It's impossible not to! I think it's an awesome coincidence. Who knows what it means for us? I guess time will tell—or maybe fate."

"Who knows. The kids in that story both ended

up dead, didn't they? From gang wars, sort of."

"It was families, not gangs, in Shakespeare. Scary enough and close enough to give me chills, though."

"We had two rival gangs at my old school. The Ramones were all Mexican-American kids, and they hated everything that wasn't deep-roasted in Spanish stuff. The other gang was all black kids—they called themselves the Black Daddies, and they were the ones that just appeared overnight, it seems. The Ramones got together when it looked like the Black Daddies were taking over the school. So when they had 'gang walks' in the halls, the Daddies would take the third floor, and the Ramones would take the second floor. Only kids that the gang approved of were safe, and no one really knew if they were on the safe list or not. Both gangs would recruit guys to fight and girls to hang with them. The girls liked the gangbangers because they always seemed to have money and cars and expensive clothes.

"What they called 'wars' would start on Friday and continue through the weekend. On Monday, the winner would 'walk' the first floor, as a sign of dominance for the week. It was a strange system, but we understood it and it worked—until Mr. Cordero. He tried to change things, and he died. Everyone was afraid. No one was learning. No one was teaching. Kids were getting hurt, so we left. Do you think my family is chicken?"

"No way, Julio. I can't believe it was that bad. I hope it doesn't get like that here. So far we only have this one gang. You're either in it or you're not. Most kids don't fool with the gang kids, but those who do are mean and scary, and it seems like they only think with one giant, demented brain cell instead of having any independent thoughts at all.

"The dudes who stopped by our table at lunch were all in the gang. They call themselves The Family or the Devildogs. All the kids in it are African-American, they all wear purple every day, and they carry heavy dog chains in their pockets. They don't do homework, and they don't do clubs or activities or any of the normal stuff kids do in school. They spend a lot of their time thinking up ways to intimidate other kids—like me and you today. It's much easier to give up your table in the cafeteria than get punched and have your food pushed on the floor. I know a girl who got jumped in front of the bus stop last week. She had made the mistake of breaking up with a Devildog. She was out of school for a week healing up."

"Romi, why do you think they were threatening us? Me, I can understand. Why you? They're black, you're black. Makes no sense to me."

"Well, the only thing I can think of is they don't like it 'cause you're *not* black. They don't know me very well, but they know my mom is big into African culture and I work at her store. But there's no way I'm gonna let them tell me who I can talk to or eat lunch with! No way!

"You know, now that I think about it, this girl came into the shop today, talking about you and me and why were eating together. I thought it was a little weird, but she was wearing purple, and I think I've seen her hanging around Terrell and his boys."

"So what do we do if they come back, Romi? There's no way I'll let them threaten you or hurt you."

"You'd protect me, Julio?"

"With my life."

"Wow. Nobody's ever told me that before! But maybe we're jumping the gun. All we had was a couple of idiots stare at us at lunch. Nobody is talking about death threats."

"I'll see you tomorrow at lunch. Good night, Romi."

"G'night, Julio. Bring the hot sauce. We may need it."

Romi hung up the phone and mused about the day's events. It was great that Julio seemed to really like her, but why all the hassle from gangbangers? Didn't they have more important battles to fight? She fell asleep, frowning about the possibilities of the future.

22.

Ben and Julio

Ben and Julio had just changed for gym class. Julio
liked gym. He had a strong upper body, plus he was
a fast runner. The girls in the class noticed his mus-
cular arms on his first day of class; the guys were
learning he could get the ball where it needed to be.
Today they were playing volleyball—lots of noise,
whacks, and an amazing amount of excitement over
getting a small white ball back and forth over a net.
"Hey! My man Julio! Give me a lunch report! This
is better than a soap opera or a talk show," Ben called
as he ran across the gym to toss the volleyball into
the basketball hoop.

"You're crazy, Ben. You can't even make a basket
with a volleyball," said Julio, laughing. "Watch how it's
done!" The ball swooshed smoothly into the net just
as the teacher blew the whistle to choose teams. Julio
and Ben sat on a bench near the back of the gym.
They let the younger kids play first since there was not
much challenge playing ninth graders. They'd play in
a few minutes when the juniors and seniors took the
floor.

"So, tell me, dude. What's up with you and Romi?"

Julio smiled as he retied his gym shoe. "Romi and I met for lunch again. She looked good—she had on this African dress with a matching scarf. She said it came from Kenya and her mom's shop. She looked like some kind of queen or something—a queen chomping on french fries."

"And now we have crowned her queen. You got it bad, Julio. What did you talk about—the crown diamonds?"

"No, stupid. We talked about puppies, and how I'd get to her house to pick one out."

"Ever been to her house?"

"No, of course not! The thought of going to her house makes me jumpy. I've been to lots of girls' houses, but Romi's family has money. I know she lives in the nice part of town out beyond London Woods."

"Yep, and Romi's house has a huge backyard, with trees and walkways, even. I've been there a couple of times. It's really phat."

"She said she had deer in her yard in the morning. Cool." The volleyball was so far out of bounds that it landed at Julio's feet. He laughed and tossed it back to the ninth grader with ease. "Toss it the other direction, kid," he called. "You get more points for your team that way." The boy grinned and returned to his game.

"So where do you live, Julio? In a dungeon?" Ben asked while he lay flat on the gym floor.

"Almost," answered Julio. "Our little place is a dull, gray apartment box on the other end of London Woods. Lots of people, more concrete than greenery, and more pigeons than deer. We only live a few miles apart, but what a difference a few miles of woods can make. So, are you going to do sit-ups or what?"

"I'm inventing a new exercise. It's called lay-downs. You don't have to move at all!"

"You're nuts!" Julio chuckled.

"Don't let where Romi lives intimidate you," Ben continued. "Go for it!" He turned on his side then. "Must exercise all parts of the body," he said with great seriousness. "So you got through the meal with no hassle this time?"

"I wish! Near the end of lunch, just before the bell rang, the Devildogs came back. There were five of them this time, all dressed in the purple hoods, silently standing at our table and staring."

Ben sat up. "The leaders of The Family! What did they say?"

"They didn't say anything. I guess they figured their silence was loud enough."

"What did you do?"

"Romi and I had already planned what we would do. It worked perfectly. We kept talking and totally ignored them—acting as if they were invisible."

"I know that pissed them off."

"Yeah, it made them really mad, and it seems like they stared even louder, if that's possible."

"So was that it?" Ben seemed disappointed.

"No. Wait till you hear," Julio replied with a mix of

excitement and mystery in his voice. "Just before the bell rang, Romi pulled her portable CD player out of her book bag, turned it up as loud as it would go, we jumped up on the table, and we started dancing."

"You didn't! I love it!" Ben rolled on the floor with delight.

"Everybody," continued Julio, "of course, turned to see what we were up to, including Mr. Prince, who headed our way from across the cafeteria. The bell rang just at that moment, we gathered our stuff, grabbed hands, and ran from the cafeteria. We were laughing so hard! Wow—that was the first time I touched her—it was like bright green electricity!"

"You held hands? Gee, take me back to kinder-garten!"

"Your nose is starting to look normal. Want me to redecorate it again?"

"Nah, man. Save it for The Family!" Ben declared, touching his nose and nose ring carefully. "So what happened to the Devildogs?"

"A friend of Romi's told her that the Devildogs were left standing by our table, looking stupid, and by the time Mr. Prince had waddled over, they had dis-persed. Mr. Prince never really knew who had the nerve to dance on his lunch table. We got away clean."

"Righteous, man. So what happens now?"

"Who knows? I hope they figured out we don't want anything to do with them. Hey, we're up to play now. Watch me serve you out!"

"After all that exercising I just did? Give me a break!" They ran out onto the gym floor, laughing.

23.

Romiette and Destiny—
Between Classes

The bell rang for the end of sixth period. The halls, which had been silent just a few seconds before, were instantly crowded with hundreds of students trying to get to seventh bell in the five minutes allotted. Most could probably make it in three, but the two extra minutes were necessary to stop by their lockers, run to the bathroom, and talk with their friends. Instead of moving the pace along, as their teachers constantly tried to encourage them to do, they huddled in noisy, excited bunches, anxious to share the last tidbit of news or gossip, which, of course, had changed in the forty-five minutes since the last change of classes.

Romi saw Destiny first. She was easy to spot. She was dressed in bright orange—pedal pushers, body shirt, and big-heeled shoes—and her hair was full and fluffy.

"Destiny! Com'ere, girl. Guess what! Julio held my hand today! We were laughing and running after we left those Devildogs in the cafeteria looking stupid, and he grabbed my hand, and oh my goodness, it felt so good!"

"My psychic powers tell me you got it bad, girl. Or you got it good. What's up with the gangbangers? Why they sweatin' you?"

"Forget the gangbangers! Julio touched me!"

"For real, girl. I see your soul mate rising out of the mist. Tell me what it felt like when he touched you. This is important."

"It felt like fire, like ice, like spice, like magic. I think he felt it too."

"Fire. Ice. True signs. He's a Pisces, a true water sign, and you're a Leo—pure fire. A joining of the opposite forces of the universe! Awesome!"

"When we got to the end of the hall, Mr. Wilkins—that substitute with the fake eyeball—walked toward us and shushed us, but he smiled, and we smiled back. Even with only one good eye Mr. Wilkins could see the sparks."

"I'm taking notes, Romi. I've got to check my star books on this one—true soul mates meet in this life, and I am here to witness it! What happened next?"

"When Julio finally let go, my hand felt empty. I got embarrassed and was afraid to look at him. He touched my hand once more, then ran to his gym class to get there before the bell rang. I heard the late bell, but didn't even notice it. I danced to French, and didn't even care when the teacher asked me, in French, if I wanted a detention for being late. I told her, 'Suit yourself,' and just smiled."

"You said that to Madame Mantua? How many detentions did she give you?"

"She must have thought I'd lost my senses, because she just told me to sit down and to come back down to the earth's atmosphere. Was it that obvious?"

"It must be something in the stars, because if I just giggle in Madame Mantua's class, she sends me out," Destiny moaned. "I've started leaving a chair in the hall so I have someplace to sit when she puts me out of class! Maybe I should fall in love too."

"Who said anything about love, Destiny? He makes me feel silly, happy, crazy—but that's not love, is it?"

"Feels the same, they tell me, but how would I know? I get all my information from star books and teen magazines."

"Hey, the bell is getting ready to ring. I gotta go. Me and Julio are supposed to talk again tonight on the computer. I'll call you after that."

"OK. Have fun up there in the stars! There's the bell! See ya!" Destiny's slim orange figure disappeared into the classroom.

"Later." Romi walked slowly down the quickly emptying hall. She was thinking of Julio, not math class, and she smiled as she shifted her book bag on her shoulder.

24.

Private Chat Room Conversation

Hola, Romiette:
Do you think those Devildogs will come after us now that we made them look stupid in front of the whole cafeteria? I'm not scared of them, but you never know how the peanut minds of people like that operate.

Yeah, I think they'll try something. They have to in order to look good in front of the others. We'd better be careful, or at least plan something just as outrageous for the next time they try to stare us down. Were you scared?

Me? Que no! I came prepared with extra weapons—Jell-O cubes in my back pocket!

Yeah, right, Jell-O kills. I forgot. Oh, I almost forgot. The puppies are old enough to go. Are you coming on Sunday?

Yes, about three o'clock. What will your

mother say about me? You know I'm a little scared about meeting your folks.

Even though there's no reason for you to feel funny, I think I know what you mean. Parents of a girl look at every dude that comes over as a somebody who will take their little darling away. My dad is going to have it really rough when I finally leave home. He and I are very close. He still calls me his little angel and lets me do almost anything. Mama is strict. She always says "No way" when I ask to go on ski trips or overnights with my friends. So I use my best little girl voice and plead to my dad. He usually tells Mama, "Aw, Lady, let the girl go. She works hard in school, makes good grades, and never causes us any trouble. Let's let her go." Mama usually gives in, and I smile sweetly to my dad. She knows what I'm doing. She's been using it on Daddy herself for years! The funny part is that the things that he talks Mama into letting me do are things involving boys or potential dangerous situations—like an overnight in a ski lodge with sleepy chaperones. He doesn't want me to grow up, but he lets me go to these pretty grown-up places. I guess he trusts me.

I can tell that you're crazy about your dad. And your mom sounds cool too. My parents are a little tighter. They're very strict on me, and expect me to do well, so

I do. I see kids all around yelling at their parents and talking back and coming in late and stuff. I wouldn't even know how to do that. I guess I'm pretty lame.

No, you don't sound lame. I get tired of hard-headed, big-headed boys who think they're so bad that they can't even take time to be nice to their mama. I like the way you talk about your folks with respect. But didn't you ever just want to run singing into the moonlight and do exactly as you wanted to do? Sky dive naked from a plane? Eat ice cream for breakfast and broccoli for dessert?

I like your attitude! Yeah, I guess I've thought about doing that kind of stuff. I'd like to swim across the Nueces River, at the widest crossing, in a thunderstorm, at mid-night! How's that?

You're getting there! Do you have clothes on for this swim? Are you carrying anything?

No, I'm naked as a newborn rat! And I'm carrying a backpack—no—two backpacks! And they're full of medical supplies, which I must deliver or the lives of the children of Mexico will be lost! And it's cold—at least fifty below zero!

Now you're talking! I think I'll be in that warm
little yacht next to you—the one with a motor
and a heated cabin and a fully stocked kitchen—
in a coat, sipping cocoa, watching you swim!

You make me do all that, and you sit sipping
hot chocolate while I freeze my naked buns?

It's your fantasy! I'm having fun watching you.

You're silly. And it's so much fun to talk
to you. Want to hear another fantasy? It's
a little scary.

I'm ready.

I imagine two sixteen-year-olds, a little
different on the outside but sharing something on the inside, on a beach. I imagine
them touching each other in the moonlight
on that beach. It wouldn't matter if it
were a thunderstorm, or a hurricane, or
fifty below zero—it wouldn't matter
because they wouldn't notice. They'd only
see each other. He would whisper soft
phrases of Spanish love songs into her ear,
and she would tremble in his arms because
even without knowing the words she'd know
the meaning, she could feel the tenderness
of his lips on hers. And the world would
stop for those few moments while they stood

there in the shadows of the night.

Wow, Julio. You have a way with words. I had
that same fantasy many nights, while trying to
get to sleep. I imagined that young man and that
girl standing on the beach, on a mountain, in
a crowded room—no longer alone, but together.
I have imagined the feel of his lips on mine.
I have imagined how safe I would feel in his
arms. I don't understand it—I don't want to.
But I know it is real and powerful and wonderful. I'm not sure what to do with these feelings—I've never felt like this before. But I
want to be with him.

Romiette, you are my dream.

Julio, my dreams are sometimes terrifying.

I will protect you.

From my dreams?

Maybe I will be there for you in your dreams.

I have to go. My mother wants to use the computer. I'll talk to you tomorrow. Call me.
Better yet—write me. I love the way you say
things. Good night.

Good night, Romiette. Sweet dreams.

25.

Dream

Romiette washed her face and quickly slipped on her pajamas. She couldn't stop smiling. She hurried to bed and snuggled under the covers onto the cool, soft sheets. She plumped two pillows behind her head, and hugged one in front of her. She reached up, turned off the light, said a quick thank-you to the darkness, and let herself think of Julio. How could someone she'd only known such a short time so completely fill her thoughts? He was clever, and kind, and smart, and oh, so good-looking. His eyes sparkled, his grin was infectious, and his voice—his voice was . . . She drifted to sleep, smiling, thinking of Julio, his voice echoing in her dreams.

They were running, fearful, in a place she had never seen. She was hot and sweating, but the air was cold. The sky was black and green with slices of bright yellow. Was that rain or blood that was pelting her, soaking her? She was crying.

He held her hand tightly, never letting it go. She could sense his fear, feel his heart beating. He was afraid for her,

*for them. Why? She couldn't remember, couldn't see through
the storm. She smelled the water then. Deep, evil, powerful.
The water was her only hope, her only chance. She
screamed, jumped, and screamed again. Then all was silence
as the water thundered into her ears, forced itself down her
throat, and burned its way into her nose, her lungs, her
brain. This water was fierce and deadly—not cool, gentle
waves but hot, choking, liquid flames, sucking the breath of
life from her. She struggled, searching for air, for land, for
something to hold on to. But there was only the water,
pulling her into its depths. She couldn't breathe. She
couldn't swim. She could no longer scream. The water filled
her, seared her thoughts, and she drifted slowly into unconsciousness. The fire cooled, the terror ebbed, and the dark
shadow of death embraced her.*

*She drifted then—in a haze of colors and swirls and
black, frightening void. Voices? Could she hear voices? One
voice? No, all was silence. No reason to care, to breathe, to
live. So easy to let the silence swallow her. That voice. It
pierced the darkness. It was calling her name, grabbing her
thoughts, and making her remember the fear, the pain, the
cold, clammy water. The water! She gasped, and the water
grabbed her once more, viciously dragging her to its depths.
But that voice. A man's voice. It floated down to where she
lay, cradled in the arms of the victorious water. The voice
called her one last time. It was Julio.*

Romiette's scream pierced the night, and she sat
straight up in her bed. She was shivering violently as
her mother rushed into the room. Her mother sat on
the bed and cuddled Romi as she had when she was

a child. She rocked her and whispered, "Romi, baby, what's wrong?"

Romi shivered from cold, and she felt wet and clammy. She gulped huge breaths of the night air. "I don't know, Mama, I had a terrible dream!" It felt good to be in her mother's arms once again. Romi slowly relaxed and started to breathe normally.

Her mother stroked her back. "Shhh. It's OK now. Let's turn on the light. Breathe easy now. That's better. Do you remember it at all?"

Romi knew every single detail, but she told her mother, "No, it's all a blur. Someone was chasing me and I fell and I don't remember anything else." Somehow she couldn't tell her mother the truth— not yet.

"Do you want me to stay in here with you?"

This time she told the truth. "Yes, Mama. Just for a little while." Romi smiled and snuggled back under her covers. Her mother smiled and curled up next to her daughter. She stayed there until Romi slowly drifted back to sleep. The dream did not return that night.

26.

At Destiny's House

Destiny and Romi were sitting on Destiny's huge water bed. They were supposed to be doing homework. They had to complete all the essentials first—fix their hair, pick out outfits for the next day, and do each other's nails. Romi, still shaky and unsettled from the dream of the night before, asked, "Destiny, you know that dream I told you about? It's back, even more frightening. More details. I'm running, running from death, then I'm drowning. And the voice, the voice at the end of the dream I couldn't identify . . ."

"It was Julio, right?" Destiny cried with satisfaction.

"Does that mean he saves me, or is he the one who's drowning me? It's so confusing!"

"Can you tell who you're running from?"

"No, it was dark and shadowy, and there was blood, or rain—I couldn't tell which—and Julio was holding my hand and we were running from—"

"Wait a minute. Julio was holding your hand while you were running?"

"Yes!"

"Then he couldn't be the one drowning you. He was the voice!"

"I don't know. I'm so confused. And scared. What does this all mean?"

"Don't worry about it now. The stars have a way of working these things out. When did you talk to him last?"

"Last night. On the computer. In our private chat room. I didn't see him at lunch today because I had to see my counselor about the SATs. But I hope I haven't screwed everything up!"

"What did you do, Romi? Did you tell him about the dream?"

"No, but I told him something else, at least I think I did."

"Told him what? You didn't tell him about the Scientific Soul Mate System, did you? I'd be *sooo* embarrassed if a dude knew we believed in that stuff."

"No, of course not. I think I told him how I feel about him. I'm not sure what I said. It's so easy to talk to him."

"What does he know for sure, girl?"

"Well, he knows I like him, want to be with him. But it's worse than that. I've never felt like this before. I feel like I want to crawl up into a little molecule and become a part of him. I never want to not be with him. Good grief—this is not me."

"You didn't tell him all that, did you? We've got to leave *something* for him to find out."

"No, I'm not stupid—but then again, maybe I am.

I can't believe I've fallen stupid head over heels in love with Julio Montague. How am I going to tell my mother? What am I going to tell her?"

"Forget your mother. Mothers are always the last to know good stuff like this!"

"You're right. Besides, there's nothing to tell yet— but I can't wait to see him. He's coming over Sunday to get the puppy."

"What time?"

"Three, I think. I'm so mixed up, I can't remember."

Destiny bounced on the water bed. "What are you wearing, Romi? This is the critical question."

"Oh, my goodness! I haven't even thought about it! My black jeans and that black sweater? No, I hate that sweater. What about your green outfit?"

"My green outfit? Yeah, you look better in it than I do. You can take it when you go home."

"No need. I already have it. But I'll take some shoes. I don't have shoes to go with it."

"You want my underwear too?" Destiny laughed.

"That won't be necessary." Romi smiled. "You know, I'm not gonna sleep until Sunday. I'm halfway scared to sleep anyway. I've got to fix my hair for Sunday too. Maybe I'll curl it and wear it down."

"What if it rains?" Destiny asked, frowning.

"It can't rain! If it's rainy, I'd better call the weather—my hair gets puffy and droopy. He seems to like it the way I usually wear it, but I'm not sure now. I wonder if Mama will let me go shopping. I need new shoes. No, it's muddy out there by the puppy cage. I'll wear yours."

"Gee, thanks."

"What difference does it make? Julio doesn't seem to mind what I wear or how I look. He said he likes me. I can't stop smiling!"

"I've got to go plot your signs and make up a love course for you. But right now, the stars are shining!"

"Yeah, but what about the dream?"

"Right now, your dreams are golden. Hang on to that."

"Should we start on this math assignment?"

"Yeah, I guess we stalled long enough."

"OK, but don't let me forget the shoes."

27.

Julio and His Mother

Julio looked out of his window to a cold, bleak rain. It had rained all day, but he didn't care. The sun was shining in his heart, in his room, in his world. The day was bright with thoughts of Romiette. Her smile, her giggles, her laughter. Thinking of her made him feel like a crayon, full of color and possibilities, a speck of color in a world of drab gray and dark rain.

Julio's mother peeked her head through his open door. Julio smiled. His mother had long black hair that showed no gray, and a face that was beautiful but somehow very sad. She rarely spoke to Julio of the three children she had buried before he was born. But he knew that she carried them with her, even in this cold and lonely place so far away from their small resting places. Julio always had been able to talk to her with ease. It was his mother he first told about the gang problem at his old school, about his anger and pain of moving, and also about his fight and friendship with Ben. Perhaps she would understand about Romi.

"Come in, Mama," he offered quietly.

"How's it going, little one, on this rainy, cold day?" she asked him.

"I didn't even notice the rain, Mama," Julio admitted. "It's a rainbow day to me."

"What's her name?" his mom asked immediately.

"What makes you think it's a girl?" Julio teased. "It could be the fact I made the jazz band."

"Jazz band doesn't bring sunshine on a rainy day, my son. Only a special someone."

"She *is* special, and her name is Romiette, Mama," Julio admitted with a smile.

Maria Montague looked into her son's eyes. "You want to talk about it?"

"I don't even know how it happened so quickly. All I know is I met her at school and I can't stop thinking about her."

"And her feelings about you?"

"Why should she care about somebody like me? She hardly even knows me. All I know is I can't stand to be away from her. Her curiosity, her sense of adventure—they all make me want to dance, or jump, or yell with excitement."

"She sounds quite special—someone worth treating with great care."

"Oh, yeah, she's all that, all right!" Julio was surprised at the amount of understanding his mother showed.

"What does she look like?" asked Maria Montague. "Tell me about her."

"She's a jewel in a pile of rocks. She's like

chocolate cake for dinner—and I *love* chocolate!"

"My goodness. She's got you talking poetry!"

"Oh, yes, Mama. The shape of her fingers, the curve of her back, the tilt of her head—all make me dizzy. I even like the sound of her voice—a little low and full of secrets. If she could put that voice of hers in a bottle and sell it, she'd be rich!"

"Well, it seems that she has one satisfied customer, at least. I'm glad you've found someone special, Julio. Take your time. Cultivate your friendship first. The romance will happen soon enough."

"I'm working on the friendship part, Mama. She's the girl I'm getting the puppy from. I'm so glad you said we could have one. I'm going to her house Sunday to get it. I wonder if her parents will be there and what they'll think of me. Maybe they won't like me."

"Of course they'll like you. What's not to like?"

"But you're my mother. You *have* to like me!" Julio grinned.

"And sometimes that's not easy!" She smiled back. "Go to her house, be yourself, and don't worry so much. If you see something golden in this girl, then her parents must have done a pretty good job of raising her, so they must be pretty special as well."

"You're sorta smart, Mama."

"I remember the feeling of young love. You feel as if you have found your dream. And you can't stop smiling."

Julio smiled. "You got that right!"

28.

Conversation—
Ben and Julio

Julio stood in the main hall of the school, waiting for the bell to ring to start the day. It seemed like years since that first day when he had rearranged Ben's face and found a friend. The halls were still as dark, the building just as ugly, but many students who had been strangers were now acquaintances whose names he remembered, and some had become friends. "What's up, Julio!" or "Hey, Julio!" greeted him as he found a place to toss his book bag and wait for the rush to get to first bell. Romi wasn't there yet, but Ben's arrival was always a surprise. Today his hair was parted in the middle. One half glowed bright pink. The other half shimmered an iridescent silver. Kids cheered in approval as Ben took his bows. Julio shook his head and grinned.

"What's up, Julio? My main drop of tequila in this concrete seashore we call home."

"Your home, man," retorted Julio. "I'm just living here till I can get back to mandolins and mariachi music."

"Hey, I don't see you buyin' no plane ticket—looks

like you're spendin' lots of time with Romiette. She seems to be makin' your sojourn here rather pleasant."

"Yeah, man. She's hot sauce for my mashed potatoes."

"Chocolate for your cornflakes!"

"Pretty poetic for a dude with two-toned hair."

"Pink and silver hair is what poetry is all about. Expression! Creativity! Besides, orange is old. That was yesterday. Gotta stay fresh, my man."

"Gotta stay alive. Don't want those Devildogs to keep hasslin' me and Romi."

"They have no poetry—they have no individuality. They're just parts of a large, dirty organism, like that alien monster thing in that *Star Trek* movie—unthinking, but very, very dangerous."

"So how do you fight stuff that makes no sense?"

"You gotta be smarter than they are, Julio. And quicker." Ben did a quick little dance step.

"Easier said than done, Ben my friend. There's been a lot in the news lately about gangs in schools. They don't have solutions either."

"Hey, Julio, did you see Channel Six last night?" asked Ben as the bell rang.

"Yeah, did you see Nannette? Now *that's* an example of no brains. Whew!"

"You got that right. For about ten minutes yesterday she was looking into the wrong camera. I guess at the commercial break they told her what to do."

"You know what, Ben? I watch Romiette's dad every night to see how the show is put together. I'd give anything to work at a TV station."

"And you get Nannette Norris as an extra treat!"

"Don't remind me. Why do you think they keep her on the air?"

"Who knows? So why don't you ask Romiette's dad for a job?"

"A job? I've never even met him. I'd be scared to death just to be in the same room with him."

"So let Romiette ask him."

"No, maybe by summer I'll get enough nerve, or I'll go down and apply for a summer intern job on my own. I don't believe in people asking for favors."

"There's the warning bell. I think I'll go to class on time today and give the teacher a heart attack." Ben jogged down the hall and around the corner. "Later, Julio!" he called out.

Julio grinned and went to his own class.

29.

Hall Conversation—
Just Before Lunch

Romiette was in a hurry. She hadn't seen Julio all day. She'd missed him earlier that morning in the front hall, and hadn't run into him between classes the way she usually did. Teachers talked extra long, or someone asked her a question, and her timing had been off all day. Just as she got to the lunchroom steps, Malaka stopped her.

"Can I speak to you, Romiette?"

"Looks like you're already doing that," Romi replied with a grimace.

"What you been up to, girl? I don't see you much at lunch anymore," Malaka challenged.

"I usually eat with Julio, Malaka. I guess the whole school knows by now." Romi wanted to rush by Malaka and up the steps, but she knew it was better to act unconcerned.

Malaka knew she was interfering with Romi's plans. She spoke slowly and with purpose. "You got that right. You know, you got the Devildogs on edge."

"Why should they care who I eat with?"

"It's a pride thing—a turf thing. You know how it is."

"No, I guess I don't. I'm minding my own business, eating my own lunch, and talking to my friend. Why should they care? And you sound like you're on their side." Romi was getting impatient.

"I'm not on nobody's side. I just figured I'd warn you that they don't like what you're doing. They wouldn't like it if you were eating with a white boy either. That's just the way they see things."

"How do you know so much how they see things? You still talking to Terrell?"

"Yeah, me and Mr. T—that's his gang name— we're pretty tight. You know how that is. I really shouldn't even be talking to you, but since we're friends—or used to be—I figured I'd let you know they're watching you."

"You still didn't tell me what they plan to do."

"I don't really know. I just know that you better stay away from places where you might be caught alone—like bathrooms and stuff."

Romi was incredulous. She gasped in surprise. "I can't believe this! Are you for real?"

Malaka was unruffled. "Real as a heart attack."

"What about Julio?"

"What about him?"

"Is he in any danger?"

"If he don't learn the rules, he might have to be taught a lesson."

"What rules? Who made up these rules? How can he follow laws when he doesn't know what they are?"

"The Devildogs don't want to hurt you, 'cause you're one of the sisters on the list. You always dressed like a sister, and hung with the sisters, so there was no problem. But now you're about to get cut off the list. And that's dangerous."

"The list? You're talking crazy." Romi was angry, irritated, and very late for lunch now.

"I'm trying to get some basic stuff into your black head. And never forget—it is black," Malaka reminded Romi. "If you get cut off the list, you got no protection."

"I never asked for any protection from some gang! I don't want it or need it." Romi was so angry she wanted to cry, but she refused to give Malaka the satisfaction.

"Suit yourself. That Mexican ain't got a chance."

"What did he ever do to you? Or to anybody black?" Romi asked in disbelief.

"Nothing. We just don't need no foreigners around here mixing it up with the sisters."

"He's not foreign! He was born in this country just like you were!"

"Doesn't matter. We don't want him here."

"You're treating him just like whites treated us! Don't you think that's a little stupid?" Romi asked, trying to appeal to Malaka's sense of reason.

"I don't make the rules. I just pass on the information. Gang rules. Gang laws. Things change."

"You sure have changed, Malaka," Romi said angrily. "You used to think for yourself."

"Now I got Mr. T to think for me, and take care of me. I like that better."

"You really like Terrell?"

"Yeah, he's got it together. He makes me feel strong and safe."

"Look, can't you see? That's how Julio makes me feel."

"You shoulda picked somebody black."

"I didn't pick him. It just happened! You don't pick who you fall for. You just fall, and when you pick yourself up, he's part of your life. Can't you understand that?"

"Look, I've already said too much. Be careful. Something is going to go down, and soon. The Devildogs have to make a statement—make a showing to the school. There's too many white kids for them to try anything, but your Mexican is the perfect target. It's nothing personal. Peace. Bye."

At that, Malaka disappeared into the lunchtime crowd. Romi stood there for a minute, musing on what Malaka had told her. "Peace?" she said out loud. "Nothing personal? What are we going to do?" She ran up the stairs to find Julio.

30.

Lunch

When Romi got to the lunchroom, most of the students had finished eating and were sitting at the tables in small groups, talking loudly, yelling, joking, laughing. Trays were strewn all over the tables, and some were on the floor. Balled-up lunch bags, broken pieces of cookie, orange peels, all decorated the tables and floors. Romiette hated the way the kids kept the lunchroom, but she wasn't a one-woman cleanup crew. She looked for Julio at the back table near the soda machine. He sat with Ben, sipping a soda. Ben, who Romi knew had study hall that bell, was making a design on his tray with Jell-O cubes.

"Hi, Julio," Romi said with a soft smile. "What's up, Ben? What in the world are you doing?"

"I'm making the world's greatest Jell-O sculpture. This may be worth lots of money one day. Where's your bud Destiny? Doesn't she have lunch this bell?"

"Destiny is probably in the volunteer room, tutoring. She likes working with the younger kids. They make me itch. Aren't you supposed to be in study hall, Ben?"

"Yeah, but I studied the hall and decided I had to get out of there. Besides, I had to check on my man Julio and your problems with our purple-wearing friends. I hate what they've done to purple. I had to get rid of all my purple hair dye because of them. Such a good color on me too."

Julio laughed. "Don't worry, Ben. There are enough other colors for you. Romi, did you eat yet?"

"I had some chips earlier. I'm not hungry," she said. "But, Julio, we have a really big problem. That gang is out to get us—to get you. You're a target, just because you're new, and you're alone. So they think. But you're not alone. You've got me."

"And me!" added Ben. "Although I have no idea what I could do to help. I see bad guys and I run the other way."

"It's always good to know your friend's got your back," Julio said with a smile.

"You'll never be alone," Ben promised. "But I'm not sure what to do."

The thought of being helpless and at the mercy of thugs made Julio so mad he wanted to bite. "What do you think they'll do? Jump me?" he said angrily. "I know how to watch my back. I can fight. And I'm not afraid. We just left a place because of fear. I'm not gonna run away like my parents!"

Romi understood his anger and frustration. She touched his arm. "Remember our silly fantasies, Julio? Maybe we need to invent a place where we'll be safe and far away from all this trouble."

Julio was still tense. He shook her hand off his arm.

"Where? On the moon? On Mars? On that moonlit beach? No, we've got to live in the real world—and they've got to let us!" He smiled at her then, and put his hand on her arm. "I won't let anything happen to you, Romi. I swear. I'd give my life for you. I told you that. I meant it."

"Ouch, Julio!" Romi laughed uncomfortably. "I sure hope you don't have to. And I was just getting the hang of hot sauce on my peanut butter sandwiches!" she joked.

Ben added, "Now that sounds like a good lunch!"

"You have potential, Romi." Julio grinned. "My long-range plan is to get you to drink hot sauce straight from the bottle!"

"Dream on, Julio!" she challenged him with a smile.

"But what do we do about the Devildogs in the meantime?" Ben asked.

"We need a clear plan of defense by Monday," Romi said sensibly.

"Maybe we can figure this out Sunday, when I come over to get the puppy, Romi," Julio suggested. "Ben, I'll call you tonight."

"She gets the house call and I get a phone call. There is no justice in this land," Ben moaned.

"She's better-looking than you." Julio grinned.

"But can she do a Jell-O sculpture?" teased Ben.

"You win in that category, Ben." Romi laughed as Ben tossed his masterpiece in the trash.

"There's the bell," said Julio. "I gotta go. I'll be over Sunday at three, Romi."

"Even my mom is getting excited about meeting you and giving you the puppy," Romi told him.

"You know, my mom was pretty understanding too," Julio mused with surprise.

"Parents do that, you know," Ben inserted into their conversation, "just so we never know what to expect. It's planned confusion."

"You got that right!" Romi agreed.

"Later, Ben," called Julio as Ben sauntered into the crowded hall. Ben waved and was swallowed in the confusion.

"I'll see you Sunday, Julio. I can't wait," Romi said shyly.

"Me either." Julio smiled, then ran to class.

31.

Saturday Night—
Destiny Spends the Night

Destiny blew through Romi's front door like a windstorm. She carried two book bags, a plastic bag full of hair curlers, two shoe boxes, a stack of CDs, and a large box wrapped in brown paper. Destiny always arrived with baggage, even if she was just stopping by to pick up an outfit or do homework. She stored much of it in her car, which was her traveling closet. Romi's mom just shook her head and let her in.

"Hey, Mrs. C.! What's for dinner?" Destiny greeted her with a quick kiss on the cheek.

"Vegetarian lasagna, Destiny—your favorite!"

"How'd you know, Mrs. C.? You must be psychic like me."

"No, Destiny, you called me yesterday and told me, remember?" Mrs. Cappelle laughed.

"Well, us psychics gotta be prepared, you know. Thanks for fixing it."

"Everybody around here likes it too. How's your mom?"

"She's fine," Destiny replied as she grabbed a soda

from the refrigerator. "She still says she's going to quit the airlines, but until I learn how to teleport myself, I need her to work there so we can travel in the summer. Expands my world vision, you know."

"How very noble of you! Give her my best."

"OK. Where's Romi?"

"Romiette is upstairs pretending to clean her room."

"I've seen it messy before, Mrs. C. I've seen your whole house messy. Actually, I think I helped mess it up last time."

"That's probably true. Get upstairs before I decide to make you wash dishes!" threatened Romi's mom.

Destiny didn't have to be warned twice. "Zooming! Later, Mrs. C.!" She ran up the steps to Romi's large and airy bedroom.

"Hey, Romi. What's up?" asked Destiny as she tossed her stuff on Romi's bed.

"What do you mean, what's up? Did you bring the package?"

"What package?" Destiny replied in mock confusion.

"Quit playin', girl. The System!"

"Thought you didn't believe in that stuff!"

"Forty-four dollars and ninety-nine cents of my money gives me the right to believe! Where is it?" Romi asked.

"Got it right here!" Destiny grinned with delight.

"Did you open it yet?"

"No—still in the wrapper. I figured that we should open it together."

"OK, as soon as it gets dark, we check it out. Did you bring the shoes?"

"Yeah, did you want the green ones? I brought the black ones just in case."

"Sweet. Now I'll wear your pants with the white shirt. Do you think this will make me look fat?"

"I don't know. Try it on. Let me see what you look like in the outfit."

"I am so huge! Julio is gonna think I'm a blimp."

"If he thought you were a blimp, he wouldn't be coming over tomorrow. Chill."

Romi slipped the slacks and shirt on, pushed her hair up off her face, and looked in the mirror. "What do you think?"

"That white shirt is kinda boring. Try the green sweater."

"That's what I had out in the first place." Romi changed quickly. They wore each other's clothes and interchanged tops and pants and shoes so often that neither of them could remember whose outfit was whose originally.

"That's the best," Destiny assured Romi. "You look just a little sweet, just a little sexy, and not fat."

"Good. That's the look I was trying for. Guess who called me just before you got here?"

"Who?"

"Malaka Grimes."

"What'd she want? Didn't she already hassle you on Friday at school?"

"She basically called to threaten me again, I guess." Romi shrugged. "'Warning me,' she called it.

She made it clear that I better stay away from Julio because the Devildogs didn't like it."

"What do they care about Julio?"

"They don't like him. They don't want us together."

"Why? What did he ever do to them?"

"Nothing. That's just it. He's new. And he's not black."

"Since when is there something wrong with being Spanish or Greek, or Martian, for that matter? You just can't tell somebody how to live their life," complained Destiny.

"You can if you're with the gangbangers." Romi sighed and sat on the bed.

"You gotta be careful, Romi. Maybe you should tell your father," Destiny suggested.

"Tell him what? That some girl who used to live down the street four years ago told me not to spend time with the new kid at school? That sounds stupid."

"Just be careful. Promise me, OK?"

"What could happen? Besides, Julio won't let anything happen to me. He told me."

"Girl, you got it bad! Hey, I checked the star book for Julio's birthday." Destiny dug down into one of her bags and pulled out a well-read, much-used astrology book. Destiny didn't even brush her teeth in the morning without first checking her book.

"What does it say?" Romi asked curiously.

"Check this out. It says he is idealistic, passionate, and poetic."

"That's Julio!"

"And it says he is drawn to magical possibilities and fiery relationships."

"That's me!"

"And it also warns of the danger of fire and water meeting. It warns you to be mindful of the consequences."

Romi looked serious. "You know, most of that stuff is so general, it could apply to anybody. We just make it apply because we want it to. But Julio and I were just talking about fire and water the other night—the two strongest forces in the universe. There's strength there too, as well as danger."

"Powerful vibes we're dealing with, Romi."

"What about the dream I've been having? Maybe we shouldn't mess with this dream stuff we bought."

"No, you will not have bad dreams tonight, because I am here, and because we have the System. The stars are with us tonight. And dreams cannot hurt us."

"Do you really believe all that stuff, Destiny?"

"Believe it? I live it!"

"Yeah, but with all of the people in the world, how can all those predictions be true?"

Destiny brushed her hair. It was a dark reddish color, and if it grew straight, it would have been down to her shoulders. But it was soft, puffy, curly, and had a mind of its own. Sometimes she braided it to "teach it a lesson," but her hair always won and would unbraid itself by the end of the day and curl into puffs of defiance. "I never question the stars—I simply trust them," she said quietly.

32.

Julio and His Father

Julio opened the front door and entered with a blast of chilly air. Spring was promised, but the evenings were still cold and damp. He carried a grocery bag and a small leash. His dad was reading the paper.

"What you got there, son? Did you bring any juice? I'm thirsty."

"Yeah, Mama said to bring some when I told her I was walking down to the store to get the dog food. You want a glass of apple juice?"

"Sure, sounds great. What's with the dog food?"

"I'm going to get the puppy tomorrow, Papa, from Romiette, the girl from school who I've been talking to. Remember? She's something really special, Papa."

"The young lady, or the puppy?"

"Very funny, Papa. Both, I guess. But I really like talking to Romiette. She makes me want to sing, and I can't even carry a tune!"

"Julio, you're not getting too involved with that girl, are you? I don't like it." He took the glass of juice and set it down.

Julio hated to disagree with his father, but there

were some things his father had no business interfering with, and one of them was Romi. He bristled with instant anger. "What do you mean, you don't like it? You don't have to like it! *I'm* the one who likes her!"

"I am your father, and you must obey me!" Even as he said it, Luis knew it sounded old-fashioned and stupid, but he felt like he had backed himself into a corner.

"You gotta be kidding! I'll obey you about doing my homework, or calling when I'm out late, but I will *not* obey you about who I see or who I care about. You can't make a rule about my likes and dislikes, just like you can't make me like bananas or not like pizza."

"Try to understand, Julio. I speak from experience," Luis pleaded.

Julio was not to be quieted yet. He was amazed at his reaction to this. He had never spoken to his father like that before. "You speak from fear! You're old! And you have forgotten what it's like to be young and happy and maybe even in love!"

"In love? Has it come to this already? You just met this girl!"

"I never said I was in love. I said you forgot what it feels like!"

"No, my son. I have not forgotten. Let me tell you a story about fear, and about forgetting. When I was a young man—about fifteen years old, and long before I met your mother—I was very much in love with a beautiful young woman. Her name was Angelina Rosina Diaz, and I knew that I would one day marry her. Her smile lit up my whole world."

"I would say that's how Romi makes me feel, but you don't want to hear it." Julio's face was set in anger. He sat on the sofa, waiting for the story he knew was coming.

"Let me finish, son. One day after school—even then there was trouble—she and I were walking home together. It was March third. I will never forget that day. Anyway, a large group of young men—college boys, we found out later—drove by us. They were very loud and very drunk. They screamed obscenities at us and chased us off the road with their car. We were terrified and ran in the ditch by the road, trying to escape that car. A fence blocked our escape across a field. They kept at us, purposely edging the car toward us, trying to knock us down. Angelina finally tripped and fell and . . . and . . . as the young men cheered, the car sped up, rolled over her, and crushed her. They drove off, then, screaming and laughing. I held the bleeding Angelina in my arms until she died."

"I've heard that story before, Papa. I know it saddened the rest of your life, but what does it have to do with me and my relationship with Romiette?"

"I know you know the tale, Julio. But did you know the young men in the car were black? I have had a fear of black people since then, and what they can do. I will not allow you to develop a relationship with one of those people!"

"'One of those people'? You think Romiette is related to those kids from a million years ago? Give me a break, Papa."

"No, but many of these black city children are somehow connected to gangs, or they know someone who is. I have read that in the paper."

"What a stupid, narrow statement!" Julio shouted. "You're putting everybody into one dirty pile!"

"What about those black gang kids in Texas? They threatened you daily. That's one reason we left, you know."

"So did the Hispanic gangs, Papa. The world is changing. Our generation looks at people as humans, not as races. Suppose everybody looked at me as just a Hispanic?"

"It is what you are."

"But I am so much more than that! I'm a musician, and a swimmer, and a person able to make my own decisions. You can't do that for me!"

"I will never sanction a relationship between you and a black girl!" Luis stood then.

Julio stood as well. He was as tall as his father. "Nobody asked you to!" he replied defiantly.

There was a pause. "I cannot help the way I feel," Luis finally admitted.

"I'm sorry you feel that way." Despite his anger, Julio really wanted his father to understand.

But, still, Luis would not budge. "You cannot do this."

"You can't stop me."

"Don't fight me on this, Julio."

"You started it, Papa," Julio said sadly. "Mama understands," he added.

"You mother is soft and full of love for you. She

refuses to see the dangers ahead. You will understand one day."

"I doubt it. Papa, what if I told you that some kids at school were treating me the same way you are acting toward Romi? Maybe they hate me just because I'm the Mexican kid that reminded them of some long-ago tragedy."

"What do you mean? Is there trouble?"

"No, there's no trouble. Nothing I can't handle. Just some bigots who think they can run the lives of other people just like you do. Why can't people just leave us alone? I just don't understand what difference it makes."

"It makes a difference to me, my son. It always will. Now tell me about this trouble at school."

"There's no trouble, Papa. Nothing at all. Believe me, I've got enough trouble right here at home."

Julio stomped to his room and slammed the door. Everything seemed so unfair, so against him. It was still raining outside. Dark tears of rain poured steadily from the blue-black sky, spilling past his window. Even the sky could find no sunshine.

He turned his stereo up as loud as it would go and let the music massage him. The vibrations thundered into his head, erasing the frustrations. He knew the music was irritating his father, but he also knew that his dad wouldn't ask him to turn it down. It would be like admitting he was annoyed. So Julio kept it loud, knowing exactly the effect it was having. He wouldn't have done that if his mother had been home. She would have quietly come in and turned it down, then asked him what was wrong. He couldn't fight with his mom. She was too gentle. His father was stubborn, just as he was, and had feelings like the bristles of a brush that scraped anyone who came too close.

Parents are estúpido! Julio thought as the rain made the outside muddy and the music made the inside tense. *What is it with old people and fear of somebody different? I'm sixteen years old, and he can't tell me what to do! They brought me here away from my friends and my school, and I'm not going to let him run my life. He's not gonna tell me who I should like or who I should see! He said Romi might be hooked up with gangs. I never imagined he could be so dumb. Romi is a human being—a beautiful, smart, fiery woman. And I don't care what my father says!*

33.

The Scientific Soul Mate System

Romi and Destiny finished the dishes and tossed a bag of popcorn into the microwave. Romi's mom peeked into the kitchen. "I love it when you come over, Destiny. It's the only time I can be sure Romi will do the dishes!"

"That's just because I don't have to run upstairs right after dinner and call her, Mom," Romi replied.

"You ought to do what we do at our house," Destiny said with a grin. "We just use paper plates!"

"Not while I have two perfectly good dishwashers eating my lasagna!" Romi's mom called back.

The two girls laughed, grabbed the popcorn, and went outside to check on the puppies. Max, the black Lab father, had little patience for his offspring, who nipped at him and chased his tail. Mandy, their mother, was watchful and nurturing, making sure each of the four puppies—two black and two gold—were within sight. Destiny and Romi fed the dogs, gave them fresh water, and played with the pups for a bit, letting them run across the backyard. At seven weeks, they tired after just a few minutes, and soon fell asleep in heaps on top of one another. Romi closed the gate and headed upstairs with Destiny. They took their showers, changed into the extra-large T-shirts they both wore to sleep in, put a CD into Romi's stereo, and finished off the popcorn. Waiting for the deep darkness of night to begin their experiment, they watched a movie and compared CD collections. Finally, Destiny could wait no longer. She picked up the brown paper-wrapped package and shook it gently at Romi.

"Romi, let's open it!" she said eagerly. "Is the door locked?"

"Who's going to come in? There's nobody home but my mom. But, yeah, it's locked."

"OK—let her rip. Let's see—what do we have here? A candle. They call it 'The Specially Scented, Sexually Enhanced Soul Mate Candle of Dreams and Desire.'"

"Hmmm, smaller than it looks in this picture . . ."

"But it smells good—raspberry—just like they said. And here's the tape. 'The Scientific, Specially Recorded, Simulated Stereo, Sexually Enhanced Soul Mate Recording. Includes sounds of nature and the human heartbeat!' Wow."

"Good grief. Sounds like overkill to me. We'll play that in a minute."

"And this is the ointment. It's called 'The Scientific Soul Mate Soothing and Stimulating Dream-Enhancing Salve of Sensuous Sensibilities.' It says, 'Use very small amount on the temples.'" Destiny was enjoying this process, but Romi was still doubtful.

"I guess so—look how small the package is." Romi squinted her eyes to read the tiny directions printed on the little tube.

"It should only take one dream to reveal everything, Romi. How many soul mates do you think you have in the universe?" Destiny replied matter-of-factly.

"OK, OK. Don't let me dump in your cornflakes. What else is in the box, Destiny?"

"The directions. It's just a typed sheet of paper. 'The Scientific Soul Mate System. Guaranteed results or your money back.' There's a tiny little asterisk here. I guess it refers to the fine print at the bottom of the page."

"What does it say?"

"I almost need glasses to read this. 'Guarantee valid only in Asia and Africa. In the U.S., guarantee valid only if package is unopened.' Can you believe that?"

"Well, so much for the money-back guarantee. Doesn't look like we got much for forty-four ninety-nine, plus shipping!" Romi lay back on her bed and laughed.

"I don't care!" Destiny insisted. "I *believe* in this!"

"Me too," Romi conceded. "Why not? Read the direction sheet."

"'Before retiring, place the Scientific, Specially Recorded, Simulated Stereo, Sexually Enhanced Soul Mate Recording, which includes the sounds of nature and the human heartbeat, into your tape player on a low setting—about one or two. You should be able to hear it, but not loudly. The essence of dreams is silence.'"

"I like that one. Go on."

"'Light the Specially Scented, Sexually Enhanced Soul Mate Candle of Dreams and Desire, being careful to use the Scientifically Designed Special Soul Mate Dream Catcher Vase that comes with it.'"

"Where's the vase?" Romi asked.

"I don't see it. There's a plastic cup in here. Is that it?"

"Yep, it says on the bottom, 'Dream Catcher— Made in Japan.'"

"Do you think we got rooked, Romi?" Destiny asked in one brief moment of doubt. "Oh, here's the notebook and special Dream Pen. Let's see what they call these. 'The Purple Pages of Passion, Persuasion, and Poetry' and 'The Purple Plume of Poetic Penmanship.' You gotta give them credit—they're creative!"

"Don't they sell these at the drugstore for forty-nine cents?"

"Not in purple!" Destiny replied with the fervor of a true believer. Then she wavered a bit. "You don't think we wasted our money, do you, Romi?"

"I'll reserve my judgment until morning, Destiny. What else do the directions say?"

"'Place a small amount of the Scientific Soul Mate Soothing and Stimulating Dream-Enhancing Salve of Sensuous Sensibilities on each temple. Only a tiny bit is necessary to capture the memory of a dream. Light the Candle of Dreams and Desire, being careful to place it in its special Dream Catcher Vase. It is important that all other lights in the room be in the off position for the Scientific Soul Mate System to work most effectively. When you awaken, be sure to record the remnants of your dream on your Purple Pages of Passion, Persuasion, and Poetry with your Purple Plume of Poetic Penmanship. Your soul mate is drifting in your consciousness—you must find him and bring him to reality."

"Oh, please!" Romi threw a pillow at Destiny. "These folks must think we're stupid!"

Destiny dodged the pillow and tossed it back with a grin. "You gotta believe, Romi. It sounds good to me. Turn the lights off. Wait—put the tape in first. OK—press play. You ready?"

"Ready as I'll ever be. What do you think of the music?"

"We turned off our CD to listen to this?"

Romi laughed. "Sounds like the music they play in the grocery store, Destiny."

"You gotta believe, Romi! You just gotta believe!" Destiny insisted.

"I believe we just threw away forty-four ninety-nine, plus shipping and handling!"

"The cost is of no importance, Romi. This is the moment of illumination. We are about to find our soul mates. Light the candle; turn off the lights. Wait! We forgot the ointment."

"It smells good—like peppermint. Oooh, it tingles!"

"OK, here we go, lights off!" Destiny flicked the

light switch on the wall. Darkness surrounded them. All was silent for a moment except for the thin music coming from the stereo.

"See anything, Destiny?" Romi asked hopefully.

"No, but the candle smells good."

"Feel a dream coming on?" Romi felt nothing. She hoped Destiny had better luck.

"Not yet. I feel hungry. Is there any popcorn left?" Destiny ate constantly and never gained a pound.

"Forget your need for food. This is much too important. Sleep now, and dream."

"How can I go to sleep?" Destiny moaned. "This is the worst music I ever heard in my life!" Destiny glanced at the digital clock radio that sat between the bed. She sat up suddenly. "Oh, my goodness! Romi! Look at the time! We almost missed it!"

"Missed what? I was almost asleep! What are you talking about?"

"Look at the clock!" Destiny squealed with excitement.

"Oh, you're right! How could I be so stupid? It's ten minutes after eleven. Are you ready?"

"Ready!"

"Here it comes—the magic wishing time—eleven minutes after eleven—11:11 on the digital clock." Destiny and Romi had been playing this game for years, even though they had long outgrown it.

They did it almost unconsciously most of the time. When the clock read 3:33, that was a chance for a wish, and again at 4:44, and around the clock. But for only two minutes out of twenty-four hours are the numbers in perfect alignment—at 11:11. These were the most powerful wishing times.

"I know what I'm wishing for!" Destiny whispered.

"Sh–sh–sh–sh. Shut up and wish, Destiny!" Romi urged. Even though she didn't really believe all this, Romi figured there was no harm in a wish, and if somebody said that was the best time to do it, then she wasn't missing the opportunity.

"I'm wishing! I'm wishing!" Destiny squeezed her eyes shut as the numbers 11:11 blinked onto the front of the clock.

"Did you wish for your soul mate to appear?" Romi asked.

"You know the rules say you can't tell your wish. If you do, it won't come true, Romi."

"I know. Destiny, did you ever catch the Fantastic Five?"

"Once I got close. I wished on 1:11, then I caught 2:22. At 3:33, I was in the bathroom, but I remembered just in time and caught it and wished before it clicked over to 3:34. Then I just sat by the clock until 4:44. I knew I had it. I wished the same wish every time.

"Then my mom made me go to the grocery store with her at 5:30. I tried to explain that I had to wait twenty-five minutes, but of course she wouldn't hear of such a thing, so I got in the store, looked frantically for a digital clock, but by the time we got out of the store, the clock in the car said 6:22. I was so upset. I've never gotten that close since."

"I've never caught more than three in a row. I wonder what would happen if you caught the Fantastic Five and 11:11 as well," Romi mused.

"They say that if you wish the same wish on all of them, it's guaranteed to be granted, plus you get a bonus wish as well—for free!" Destiny said with authority.

"Sounds like extra credit in school."

"Hey, Romi, did you ever wonder who 'they' is? You know, how 'they' say something will happen, or 'they' think the world is changing?" Destiny asked.

Romi flopped back on her pillow and grinned at the darkness. She and Destiny often had the same weird questions, and this was one she had considered often. "Yep," she said, "I think I figured it out. The 'they' that everybody talks about as experts on everything is *women*!"

"Women?" Destiny repeated.

"Yeah. Men will never admit that women know everything, so when you hear the statement that 'they' say the ozone layer is disappearing, you'll know it's a woman's opinion being quoted by men!"

"I like that! One day I'm gonna catch all those times on the clock," Destiny promised herself.

"I wonder what 'they' will say."

"'They' will say that history has been made—finally!"

"By a woman, of course!" added Romi.

"Of course! Good night, Romi. Dream on!"

"The last time I talked to Julio on the computer, he signed off with 'Sweet dreams'!"

"See there, you're guaranteed no bad dreams!"

"Destiny?"

"Yeah?"

"Thanks."

"For what?"

"Nothing. Everything."

"G'night, Romi."

"G'night, Destiny. Julio's coming over tomorrow!"

"Sleep!"

"OK!"

34.

Sunday Morning

Destiny woke up first. She looked around, glanced at the clock, and tried to remember if she had dreamed at all. She felt mellow and well rested, and she seemed to remember music—not the tinny tape from last night, which mercifully had shut off after thirty-five minutes, but loud, powerful, stimulating music. Then she remembered. "Romi, wake up! I saw him! My soul mate!"

"Who?" Romi asked groggily. She always slept hard and she didn't awaken easily like Destiny. Romi didn't like early mornings. And lately, she didn't like dreams either.

"My soul mate," Destiny insisted. "The System works! What about you? Did you dream of Julio? What's wrong?"

"I'm not sure. I did dream—but it's hazy and unclear."

"Was it Julio? Is he your soul mate?"

"Yeah, I did dream of Julio, but it wasn't a good dream," Romi said slowly, trying to remember. "It was the same dream again. We were running, and there was water all around, except this time there was fire too. The water was on fire, I think. We were both screaming and . . . I don't know. I can't remember anything else. Maybe that stupid system does work. But I thought it was supposed to give you a good dream. What's all this stuff about fire and water?"

"That's proof it works!" declared Destiny. "Don't be afraid. Your star signs are fire and water. I knew the Scientific Soul Mate System was worth the money!"

"Destiny, I've been having that same dream for weeks now—for free!"

"No, Romi, you had it this time because of the candle and the music and the ointment." Destiny was determined to be a believer.

"What about you, Destiny? You dreamed about your soul mate?"

"Yes! I saw him! But I'm not sure what he looks like. I kept seeing this rainbow. Colors all around. Red, blue, bright orange. The rainbow kept me from seeing his face clearly. But I could tell he was fine— so fine! And I think he had freckles." Destiny got out of bed and danced around the room.

"Freckles? Was he black?"

"I don't think so, but I'm not sure. I remember something else. There was music. Lots of music. Loud, glorious, clanging music. And opera music."

"Maybe you will get to the prom after all. Opera music? That was a nightmare!" Romi scratched her head and yawned.

"I don't think this was prom music. I think I'll have to expand my musical appreciation to opera too, because this dude is just too fine to pass up. I'll educate him about real music later."

"What's his name?"

"I'm not sure, but I know he's a Taurus—or maybe his name is Taurus, or Tauran—something like that. But he's strong like a bull, and you know that Taurus is the only sign I can marry, because that is my only cosmic match, and there are *no* boys in Cincinnati who fit the description!"

"That's what you say. Where does this dude live, Destiny?"

"I will meet him in London."

"London? When will you get to England?

"Doesn't matter. Doesn't matter. He will wait for me until I get there. He knows of me and is waiting now. It might be months, but I will know him when I see him. And he will know me. Just like you and Julio."

"I like your faith. But the prom is just a few months away."

"I may have to go to the prom with a lesser soul. In the meantime, I better find out where I can take music lessons. I must be ready for when my true soul mate comes into my life." Destiny sighed with acceptance.

"Speaking of ready—looks like I'm gonna get good weather for this afternoon, and I only have eight hours to get ready!"

"Sorry I can't stick around, but I promised Mom

I'd let her take me shopping this afternoon after church." Destiny gathered up her bags.

"You're so kind to her."

"Yeah, she needs me. What else would she do with her money if she didn't have me? Call me after Julio leaves. I want to hear every single detail!"

"You got it!"

Destiny dressed quickly and ran to the kitchen. "You got any doughnuts?" she yelled up the stairs to Romi.

"Look on the second shelf of the refrigerator," Romi called down.

"Got it. Thanks, Romi! See ya! Call me tonight!"

"You get the first report with all the juicy details! Promise!"

With that, Destiny breezed out the door to her car.

35.

Sunday Afternoon

Romi checked the mirror one last time, then checked again. Her hair was perfect, makeup understated, her clothes casual but enticing. She had changed six times that afternoon, but just as she predicted to Destiny, she ended up wearing Destiny's green outfit. Destiny's red hair seemed to fight with the green sweater and slacks. But Romi's soft brown hair and golden brown skin complemented the green. She had brushed it back and held it with a hair comb. It looked casual and unplanned, even though she had worked for that look for hours. Satisfied finally, she went downstairs, checked to see that the dishes were put away, the counters were clear, and the living room neat and tidy. Max, the black Labrador retriever, had slipped in the back door. She chased him out and wiped up the floor where he'd left paw prints. She even ran the vacuum. Her mother watched in mild amusement. Romi had never shown this much interest in the cleanliness of the house.

"Everything looks fine, Romi," she called. "Just relax, dear."

"I don't want him to think the wrong thing about us," Romi told her mother. "I want everything to be just right," she added as she fluffed a pillow on the sofa.

"This young man must be really something, Romi."

Romi smiled broadly. "Oh, Mom, he is. I don't know why or how, but he makes me feel like I can fly."

"You met him at school?"

"Well, it's a long story, but yes. He's a transfer student from Texas," Romi answered. She knew that trying to explain all the details of how they first met on-line would cause too many questions from her mother.

"New students from other places are always fresh, and so much more interesting than the kids you see every day, right?" her mother said. "And if the new student is a boy, then fireworks are likely to happen. Am I right again?" Mrs. Cappelle smiled.

"You're pretty smart for an old lady, Mom," Romi teased. She dodged as her mother tossed a sofa pillow at her.

"You'd better watch it, kid," she warned. "This old lady is armed!" They chased each other for a moment, laughing and giggling. They landed together on the sofa just as the doorbell rang.

"He's here!" Romi touched her hair again.

"So open the door," her mom said, pushing her toward the door.

"You open it, Mom!" Romi insisted. "I don't want to look like I'm too anxious."

"OK, if you insist." She made a face at Romi,

opened the door, and smiled graciously at the nervous young man standing in front of her.

"Good afternoon, Mrs. Cappelle. I'm Julio Montague."

"Come on in, Julio. Romi is expecting you. Get down, Max," she said to the big black dog who greeted Julio as if he were his best friend. "Max knows how to open the back door, and he keeps sneaking inside to get away from his kids, I guess. Max is our retriever daddy. He's not much of a watchdog—much too friendly and lovable. Mandy, the mom, is out back with the puppies. She's a golden retriever. Have you had a retriever before?"

"No, I had a German shepherd back in Texas, but we had to leave her when we moved." Julio was glad the dog was there. He rubbed the dog's fur, grateful to have something to do. Max, of course, was pleased to have so much attention.

"That must have been rough. What part of Texas are you from, Julio?" Mrs. Cappelle looked around for Romi, who had disappeared into the kitchen.

"I'm from Corpus Christi. All my relatives are from Mexico, but I was born in the U.S."

"That's really interesting. So I guess you—oh, here's Romi—your friend from school who wants the puppy is here, Romi." Romi completely ignored her mother. She didn't notice that Max had gotten into the house. She saw only Julio. She smiled.

"*Hola,* Julio," Romi said, trying not to act as nervous as she felt.

"*Hola,* Romi. I like that outfit. You look like a beautiful flower—*¡una flor hermosa!*"

"Thanks, Julio. You always say things so . . . so fancy! It's really cool." Romi blushed, pleased that he noticed, and pleased that he thought she looked good.

"When I see you, I see poetry," he whispered low enough so her mother wouldn't hear.

Romi grinned. "Wow, you're too much! I'm gonna have to keep you around! Mama, we'll be in back." Romi headed with Julio toward the back door. Her mom was collecting her keys and purse.

"That's fine, dear. I'm on my way to the shop. I just have to do a little paperwork, so I should be back by six. We'll have dinner then, OK?" She picked up her briefcase and paused at the front door. "Lock the door if you leave the house—call me if you need to. You two behave yourselves, you hear me?"

"We're just looking at puppies, Mom," Romi declared innocently.

"You say puppies. I hear poetry. I wasn't born yesterday, you know." Her mother gave her a smile.

"OK, Mom. I know what you're saying." Romi was glad her mother was so perceptive. It was easier than having to tell her everything. Lots of times she just depended on her mother's intuition to figure things out. Then they'd talk about it.

"Give me a hug, Romi. If you keep grinning like that, your face is gonna pop! Call me at the shop, OK?" Mrs. Cappelle seemed pleased that her daughter was so happy. Julio watched the two of them closely.

"OK, Mama." Romi couldn't hold in the smile, even though she tried.

"See you later. I've got to get to the shop now. Bye." She left, and they could hear her car pulling out of the driveway. Julio and Romi were alone in the kitchen, with Max wagging his tail cheerfully between them. Romi smiled as they headed out the back door to the pen where the puppies were kept.

The four puppies started yipping and jumping as soon as they saw Julio and Romi head their way. Julio grinned as soon as he saw them. "Oh, they're awesome—two black ones and two gold. It's hard to decide. I know I want one of the gold ones. Oh, this one is so small." He picked up the smallest puppy and cuddled it in his arm.

Romi nodded. "I knew you'd pick that one." She reached for one of the black puppies. "Come here, puppy. Oh, you're so soft. I can't bear to part with them, Julio. I want to keep them all, but six dogs is too much even for me, the dog lover. And my mom is about at her limit. I was the one who convinced her to let Mandy have one litter before we got her spayed. So what shall we call your little one there?"

"How about Taco!" suggested Julio as he let the little dog run.

"Perfect! She's the same color as a little taco shell!"

Both were quiet for a moment, watching the puppies romp and roll in the grass. Finally Julio spoke. "Your mom seems really nice. I can tell the two of you are really close. Do you think your mom approves of me?"

"She liked you—I can tell," Romi assured him. "And she smiled that 'I know what's going on' smile at me. She knows me pretty well."

"Does she approve?" Julio wanted to know.

Romi thought for a moment. "She doesn't disapprove. She trusts me."

Julio frowned, remembering the words that had passed between him and his father. "I had a big argument with my father last night." His father's words and stiff refusal to change still made Julio angry.

"About what?" Romi asked gently.

Julio sighed. "You. Me. Life. Fear. Stuff like that."

"Why about me? He doesn't even know me."

"I know. That's what I told him. But he's set in his ways, and he is afraid. We left Texas because of fear."

"I'm not afraid of fear, Julio," Romi said clearly. "Your father will learn to understand."

"I hope so." Julio sighed. "We don't talk very well together." They closed the gate to the dog pen and carried the puppy into the house. It seemed content to rest in Romi's arms, and never looked back at the family it was leaving. Julio looked around at Romi's house. "You have an awesome house," he remarked. "I didn't think it would be this—"

"Big? Yeah, it's pretty big," Romi admitted. "We moved here about five years ago. I don't think about it—it's just home."

"It reminds me of my grandfather's house—big and airy and full of love."

"The grandfather with the seven wives?" teased Romi.

"Only one at a time!" retorted Julio. "Will you walk me halfway home, Romi?" he asked. "This has really been live, and I don't want it to end yet."

"Sure," she replied, "let me get my jacket. Look, Taco fits in the pocket! Have you got food and stuff?"

"Yeah, I bought puppy chow and we found an old blanket. Little Miss Taco here is even gonna sleep with me!"

"I'm not gonna even *touch* that line!" Romi laughed. "Let's go."

Julio stopped by the door. He looked directly into Romi's face. She met his gaze with a smile. "I like your smile," he said quietly. "And you're very pretty when you laugh."

Romi tried not to blush. She didn't want him to know how much like Jell-O her insides felt. "I have got to keep you around," she quipped. "You make me feel good!" She tried to change the subject. "It's a cool day, but you can tell spring is coming. You'll like it here in the spring. Everything is pale green and yellow, and even the air smells good."

That made Julio think of home. "You ought to see Corpus Christi in the spring," he countered. "Things grow there that Cincinnati hasn't even discovered yet! You'd love it—full of color and brightness, just like you!"

They headed out the door and into the cool sunlight. It was March, which meant it could snow, or it could be seventy-five degrees. But the day was brisk, and their jackets felt good. A hint of green dusted the ends of the branches. They walked quietly, in front of a long bank of trees that led to thick woods behind. They took turns holding the puppy, laughing as she chased leaves when they put her down.

"I like to walk this way," mused Romi. "This area is called London Woods. It's what's left of what was probably acres of forest back when the world was young. It's all the developers left when they built these houses. I like to come down here in the summer and listen to the trees."

"Do the trees talk to you, Romi?" asked Julio seriously.

She didn't seem surprised by his question. "Yeah, you know, they do! You know what I mean. I like the breezes and the silence."

"I can feel the magic in the air and the breezes too," Julio admitted. "But that's just not something you tell the kid who sits behind you in history class. It's the kind of thought I usually keep to myself."

"I knew you'd understand," said Romi. "There's so little left of natural stuff in the world." They looked at the trees together and listened as the branches whispered. "Destiny says you are magical and passionate. She's into star signs. You believe in that stuff?"

"It's hard not to believe when Destiny's around!"

"She's a trip, for sure," said Romi, "but she keeps the ride interesting."

"She's a lot like Ben," Julio replied. Both of them are kinda free-spirited in their own way. It's hard to fit either of them into an ordinary box."

"You got that right." Romi smiled. "It's nice having company for my walk."

"Do you often walk down here by yourself? Are you sure it's safe?"

"It's only a couple of blocks from home, and I usually have Max with me."

"Max the wonder dog? The watchdog that hugs the robbers first and barks later?"

"I see you've got Max's number," Romi laughed. "But at least he's good company for a walk in the woods."

"Better than me?"

"No, you're better, because you don't stop and pee on every tree."

"I could, if you like."

Romi giggled. "No, but thanks for offering." They laughed and had almost reached the halfway point—where Romi would leave Julio and go back home.

Julio glanced behind them. "Hey, Romi, do you see that car? It's driving awfully slow."

She turned to look. "I'm not sure. Wasn't it behind us on the last block?"

"I think you're right. Let's hurry up. My house is still a couple of blocks away. We'll go there. I'm not letting you walk home alone."

"Julio, they're following us. I can't see in the windows—they're blacked out."

"It doesn't look good, Romi," said Julio, but then he tried to ease her fears and said, "but it's broad daylight on a Sunday afternoon. We should be OK."

"But there's nobody out, Julio. Nobody walks anymore. And that car is still there!"

"Just keep looking straight ahead." They walked faster and tried not to show their fear. "Should we try to find a pay phone?"

"There's one about two blocks down, but there's nothing here but trees and woods."

Just then the car stopped. The four doors of the black Cadillac opened at the same time. As if on cue, four purple-hooded youths eased out of each door simultaneously. They slammed the doors shut in unison as well. It was well rehearsed, and as intimidating as they meant it to be. They walked slowly toward Romiette and Julio. They all wore dark shades, and none of them smiled. They did not speak—they just stared. Only the puppy seemed unconcerned by the scene unfolding. She was asleep in Julio's pocket.

Romi was frightened, but refused to let it show. She whispered, "What should we do, Julio?"

"Relax," he whispered back. "Don't act scared."

"I'm not that good an actress!"

Finally the tallest boy spoke. It was the same one who had threatened Julio in the bathroom that day. "What's up, man?" he said to Julio, looking at him as if he were gutter trash.

"Nothing much," Julio replied, his voice steady. He was more angry than frightened at this point.

"You in trouble, Romiette?" the purple-hooded boy said to her. "Yo' mama know you out with this foreigner?"

"Mind your own business, Terrell!" Romi retorted.

Julio could barely control his anger. "You're the one who's gonna be in trouble! Me and Romi ain't got nothin' to do with you!"

"Shut up, Tex-Mex," Terrell replied.

"Leave us alone, Terrell," yelled Romi. "Who I walk with is none of your business!"

"I was just checkin' on your safety, Romiette," Terrell replied slowly. "I just want to tell you that it might be safer to walk alone, you know what I'm sayin', instead of walking with whatever trash is blowin' on the street, you know what I'm sayin'?"

"Don't you threaten her!" Julio was ready to fight.

"And what you gonna do about it, Tex-Mex? You can't beat us. And we checked with our boys in Texas and found out you ain't in no gang. You ain't got no protection at all now, man." Terrell knew he had the upper hand.

"I ain't afraid of you!" Julio yelled. "Just watch me wipe you all over this street!" Julio knew he would get destroyed, trying to fight four boys at once, but his anger had taken over his reason, and he hated feeling weak and helpless. He wanted to protect Romi and he wanted to hurt those purple-wearing thugs. He lunged toward Terrell.

Julio was met by the barrel of a gun in his stomach. He inhaled and stood very still.

Terrell grinned with victory, but no laughter was in his face. "Hey, look at Tex-Mex! Tryin' to fight me! Back off, Tex. Fists ain't no match for the steel of this gun here."

Julio backed slowly away from the gun. His reason

had returned suddenly. His anger remained, but he was no fool. "You can't do this!" Julio declared. "I'll fight *all* of you!"

Romi, trembling and quiet, hoped Julio wouldn't try.

Terrell waved the gun at both of them. "Don't even try it, Tex. We packin'. All of us. So just stand there in the dirt and listen. This wasn't planned to be no killin', but it could be. Don't make this be more than it's s'posed to be. You know what I'm sayin'? Stay away from Romiette, or we'll hurt you. That's a promise. And Romi, if you continue to hang with Tex-Mex here, we can't promise to protect you anymore."

"I don't want your protection!" she shouted. "Just leave us alone and crawl back in the hole you came out of!" Terrell laughed his humorless laugh and breathed his hot breath directly in Romi's face. She didn't flinch as he stared. She just looked at him with eyes of anger and frustration. Then, with one swift lunge of his arm, he pushed her down into the dirt.

"Oops, there goes the neighborhood!" mocked Terrell. "Looks like Romi tripped and fell! Better be more careful, Romiette. This is a warning. We don't play."

Julio could take no more. "Don't you *touch* her!" he shouted. He tried again to lunge at Terrell, but the other three Devildogs stepped in and held Julio back.

Terrell put the gun in Julio's face. "Don't make me use this," he warned. "We outta here. We done said what we had to say."

They walked slowly back to their car, knowing they wouldn't be chased or stopped. They opened the four doors together, slid into the seats, and closed all four doors in unison. They drove off in a clutter of dust and road debris, tires screeching. Then all was silent.

Romi was crying now.

"You OK, Romi?" Julio asked gently.

"Yeah, I'm fine, but I'm scared enough to pee, and mad enough to spit!"

"I'd like to do more than spit. Why are they sweatin' us?" Julio could still smell the steel of that gun in his face.

"Let's get out of here, Julio. Just take me home, please."

"Sure, Romi," Julio replied. "You know, the only one who never noticed a problem was little Taco here. She slept through the whole thing."

She took the dog out of Julio's pocket and stroked its soft, silky head. The softness and calm security of the puppy soothed Romi, and gradually her heart stopped racing.

"Do you think we should we tell your parents, Romi?" Julio asked. He was still furious—partly at what the gang had done to their afternoon, and partly at his inability to fight back.

"If we tell my dad, he'll call the police and put it on the news. We do *not* want any public attention given to this. Their payback wouldn't be done in the brightness of a TV studio," Romi reasoned.

"And if we tell my dad, that would just give him

reason to make sure we don't see each other. He thinks everybody is somehow involved in a gang. He read it in the paper somewhere." Julio sighed.

"There's got to be a way for us to work this out ourselves, Julio," Romi said without much conviction. "If we go to the police, it's only a matter of time before they get one of us for it."

"You're right. I've seen it happen in Texas. Kid goes to police one week. Next week same police find that kid dead," Julio said soberly. "We have to figure out a way to stop them without involving the authorities."

"But how, Julio?" Romi moaned.

"I don't know, Romi. Not yet." Julio frowned. The wind had turned cold, and the sun had disappeared behind the clouds.

"They all had guns, Julio!" Romi whispered.

Both were silent as they walked back to Romi's house. The puppy, unconcerned, slept soundly in Romi's arms.

36.

The Six O'clock Evening News—Sunday

—Good evening. It's six o'clock on Channel Six, and this is the news. I am Cornell Cappelle, and with me is Nannette Norris. Good evening, Nannette.

—Hello, Cornell. I like your tie. In the news tonight, your taxes are going up, the temperature is going down, and we'll have a report on the new ride coming to King's Island, which goes both up and down.

—Thank you, Nannette. Also tonight we will begin our special report on teenage gangs in our cities. Who joins these gangs? What danger do gangs pose? And what is the potential for gang violence here in Cincinnati?

—Surely we don't have to worry about gangs here in Cincinnati, do we, Cornell? We've taught our kids to "Just Say No!" We've got great kids here. But other cities—they don't seem to be quite as lucky.

—That's part of what we're trying to find out, Nannette. Our city is certainly not immune. In other news, we'll look at the problem of the buildup of nuclear weapons in Third World countries, and the problems caused by this recent move to increase nuclear proliferation.

—And I'll have my report on the problems of too much peanut butter in our diet, as well as an interview with a farmer who found a frog with two heads.

—Let's pause here for a station break. I'm Cornell Cappelle, and we'll be right back.

37.

Monday at Lunch

The bell rang for lunch, and Romi, for once, was hungry. She hurried up the steps to the cafeteria so she could beat the long lines. She grabbed a salad, a bag of cashews, and an apple juice, and paid for it just as some ninth-grade boys stormed into the lunch line. They had just left gym, and it was noticeable. Romi thought she had never smelled anything so disgusting—dozens of sweaty boys crowded into a hot cafeteria. She hurried to a table in the back. Ben was already sitting there, legs propped up on the table, his blue hair in braids this time, wearing a T-shirt that read, SAVE THE WHALES. He was sipping a soda and, from the wrappings on the table, had already eaten several snack cakes and bags of peanuts.

"Hey, Ben," Romi called. "Your usual healthy lunch, I see."

"Carbohydrates are my life," Ben declared as he reached into his book bag and grabbed a bag of potato chips.

"Your blood vessels are simply going to explode one day, Ben," Romi joked. "And how do you manage to skip study hall so successfully and eat lunch with us every day?"

"It's easy." Ben grinned. "I simply ask to go to the bathroom, and I don't come back!"

"Don't they look for you, or wonder why you haven't returned?"

"It must be because I blend into a crowd so well—they just never notice!" Ben chuckled as he dug into the bag of chips.

Romi sprinkled the cashews over the salad, added a dab of dressing, and on the first stab into the food, broke the little plastic fork that came with it. "I hate when that happens!" she complained. She went to the line and got a replacement, but not without an argument from the lunch lady, who was sure that only one plastic fork per student was allowed. Romi took two and walked away.

Destiny ran breathlessly to the table and tossed her book bag under it. She always brought her lunch because she didn't eat meat and the cafeteria didn't always serve food she thought was palatable. She unloaded three plastic food containers, a thermos of soup, a thermos of juice, an apple, and a plastic bag with silverware and a napkin. "What's up?" she said finally. Ben watched her with awe.

"Do you do this every day?" Ben asked in amazement.

"Do what?" Destiny replied as she poured her soup into the thermos cup.

"Bring your kitchen in your book bag."

"I believe in taking care of this temple, my body,

because I am the goddess who lives in it."

"I like your attitude, Destiny." Ben grinned with admiration. "Do you ever eat junk food?"

"Only on weekends," admitted Destiny with a laugh. "Hey, Romi, where's Julio?"

"Here he comes," Romi answered as Julio smiled at her across the cafeteria. His long legs carried him across the large, noisy room quickly, and he plopped into the chair across from Romi.

"*Hola, amigos,*" he greeted everyone, but his eyes were on Romi.

"Hi, Julio." Romi smiled. "How's the puppy?"

"When I called you last night after I finally got home from our 'adventure,' she was scared and whimpering, but she's fine now. When I left for school, she was asleep on my bed. My mother's gonna have a fit when she finds her there."

"Moms love puppies," Ben said. "Don't worry."

"Yeah, we've got enough to worry about." Destiny sighed.

"So what *are* we gonna do about the Devildogs?" Julio said finally.

"Maybe we should tell a teacher or something," Destiny suggested.

"Right, Destiny," Julio snorted. "Like they're going to call a parent conference and tell the bad kids to be good kids, kiss them on the forehead, and send them out to sin no more. No way."

"Julio is right." Ben nodded. "Nobody is going to listen to us or be able to do anything. We've got to solve this ourselves."

Romi tossed her trash into the wastebasket. She sipped her juice and thought for a moment. "Sure, Ben," she said finally, "I can just see you walking up to the Devildogs and saying, 'Hi! I'm Ben! I've got purple hair and a kind heart. Can I talk to you guys about some problems we've been having with your gang?'"

Ben pretended to fall out of his chair. "They'll take my kind heart out and wrap it up in my purple hair. Purple is their color though, right? That's why I haven't dyed my hair any of those truly beautiful violet shades since they came around."

"Somehow," laughed Destiny, "I think purple hair is not the purple the Devildogs are looking for, Ben. We need you alive."

Julio sighed. "I've had experience with gangs. I know the only way we can stop them from sweatin' us is to make it so it's not fun or safe for them to do it."

Romi nodded. "We've got to be smarter than they are. The four of us have got to be smarter than a bunch of thugs."

Destiny cleared away her lunch containers and tossed them back into her book bag. She fixed her lipstick, checked her hair, and chewed a piece of gum to sweeten her breath. Destiny always wanted to be prepared, just in case her soul mate should walk around the corner. "I've got an idea!" she said finally.

"Does this have anything to do with the stars, Destiny?" Ben wondered.

"Well, sort of. According to my charts, the next three days are destined to be full of danger and excitement."

"Danger for who? For you?" asked Ben.

"Well, actually," Destiny admitted, "it's predicted for Julio and Romi. My chart says I should start a new diet!"

"Thanks a lot," Julio chuckled. "You risk *our* lives with your chart."

"It's all perfectly safe, I think," continued Destiny. "There was one part I couldn't figure out. I have to get the advanced book for that."

"You *think?*" Ben asked.

Romi wanted to trust Destiny's books, charts, and hunches. "Let her finish. What's your idea, Destiny?"

"Romi, your dad's station is doing a series of reports on gangs in the U.S., and the possibility of gangs here, right?" Destiny started.

"Yeah, they are. TV stations are always the last to know," Romi answered.

"I can't believe they've just figured out that gangs might be here. We know that they are!" added Ben.

"Anyway, what does Romi's dad have to do with this?" Julio wanted to know.

"Ben calls your dad, Romi, and tells him of his suspicions about kids being in gangs at our school, and gets him on the case."

"I'm with you so far. Dad would love to do that," Romi said. "Go on, Destiny."

"Then Romi's dad and his Secret Six investigative news team follow the Devildogs with a hidden camera, catch them threatening Romi and Julio, then expose it on TV. When your dad finds out it's you, the cameras will already be rolling, and he can't blow his cover or you might get hurt."

Romi shook her head. "My dad would never agree to use me to catch them. It's too dangerous."

"You're right," admitted Destiny. "But it sounded good for a moment."

"Maybe your idea can still work, Destiny," Julio said thoughtfully. "We know that gang kids like that work best in secret, right?"

"Right," agreed Ben. "They don't want their mamas to know what they do. Exposure might destroy them."

"It might destroy us too," Romi added gloomily.

"What if *we* did the filming instead of your dad?" suggested Julio.

"I'm not sure, Julio. First, it's dangerous; second, it's stupid; and third, we don't have a camera," Destiny reasoned.

"This is where Ben of the multicolor hair comes in. What about my new Minicam?" Ben was unbraiding his hair. It was now not only blue, but curly.

"What Minicam, Ben?" Julio asked.

"My dad got it for me for Christmas when he was in Japan. It's small enough to fit in a pocket and tapes both video and audio. Picture's not real clear, but it's effective."

"Let me get this straight," Romi said. "We tape them hasslin' us, and use the tape against them? And they're just going to stand there and let us do it?"

"The camera will be hidden." Ben was becoming doubtful of his own plan.

"Where?" demanded Destiny.

"In my pocket," Julio declared with finality. "I will tape these suckers and get this over with."

Ben said, "You said you always wanted to be a TV man, Julio. Here's your chance!"

"This wasn't exactly what I had in mind, though," Julio said quietly. "This is dangerous. But the way I see it, we have no choice. This way, we have proof of their threats and we can take the tape to Romi's dad and have the gang exposed. Romi, are you willing to do this?"

"I trust you, Julio. And we won't be alone. We've got Ben and Destiny for backup," Romi added.

Destiny looked at Ben; Ben looked at Destiny. Both burst out laughing at the same time. "We got your back, girlfriend!" Destiny declared.

Ben tried to get serious. "Let's get our plan straight now. Romi, you and Julio walk near London Woods again tonight—just like yesterday. Don't go into the woods—we have to be able to see you. Me and Destiny will be right behind you at all times in my car."

"What about my car?" Destiny asked. "It's cuter than yours."

"Be for real! Your car is bright red with flowers and butterflies all over it. We don't want them to notice us, remember? Now *my* car is small and brown and ugly. I never get traffic tickets. I just blend in with the scenery."

"And I have to ride in that?" Destiny sighed, and rolled her eyes at Romi.

"What if something goes wrong?" Romi asked seriously.

"We've got the car phone and we'll call for help at any time," Destiny assured her.

"I don't know, Destiny. I have a bad feeling about this." Despite her talk, Romi had never really done anything dangerous in her life. She was scared of what they were about to do, but she was more afraid to go to the authorities. She felt that Julio was probably right about gang retaliation. They had no choice. "I'm scared, Julio." She looked directly into his eyes.

"I won't let anything happen to you, Romi. I swear." Julio touched her hand gently. "But we've got to end this."

"You're right, I know. Let's do it."

Ben looked to the far end of the cafeteria. The Devildogs, seven of them, marched into the room. They worked the tables, quietly collecting chips, soda, and sandwiches from students who offered no resistance. The teachers who were cafeteria monitors noticed nothing. A young man in purple would stop at a table, smile, make pleasant conversation, and smoothly pocket a sandwich from each person at the table. Those students never smiled. They just paid their "lunch fee" to the gang and sighed with relief when they left.

The seven boys headed to the back where Ben, Romi, Destiny, and Julio were sitting. It was almost time for the bell.

"Here they come," Ben warned. "Destiny, talk loud so they hear us!"

Destiny gave it her all. She stood up next to Romi and said as loud as she could, "ROMI, GIRL, YOU AND JULIO ARE THE BOMB! HE'S COMING OVER AGAIN TONIGHT AT SIX?

GO ON, GIRL. JULIO, IF YOU HAD A CAR, YOU WOULDN'T HAVE TO WALK BACK AND FORTH PAST LONDON WOODS WITH ROMI EVERY NIGHT, YOU KNOW. SEE Y'ALL. I GOTTA GET TO CLASS." She gathered her book bag and headed for the cafeteria door. She didn't look back. The Devildogs turned abruptly and left through a side door.

"That was Destiny—loud and effective," declared Romi.

"Did they hear?" Julio asked.

Ben laughed. "They had to hear. You could hear Destiny's big mouth in Egypt. Yeah, I saw them look at each other and give a sign before they left."

"We're on for tonight," Julio said with a tightness in his voice.

"And I haven't got a thing to wear!" Ben cried, trying to lighten the mood. Nobody laughed.

"Let's meet at my house at five," Romi said. "My mom should be gone to work by then."

"Don't forget the camera, Ben," Julio reminded him.

"Gotcha!" Ben replied. "There's the bell." He gathered his gear and left.

"I'm still scared, Julio," Romi murmured.

"I know. Me too. But after tonight it will all be over and we can think about important stuff like pizza, or puppies, or prom."

"I hope you're right. See you this afternoon."

"*Adiós,* Romi. Take care." They left by separate doors.

38.

Monday—5 P.M.

Mrs. Cappelle was running late. Every Monday she left for the shop at three-thirty when Romi got home from school. She liked to be there when the afternoon shipments arrived. But she had misplaced her keys, and lost half an hour until she checked outside by the dog pen. Max loved keys and had them safely by his side. Romi checked her watch, hoping her mother would hurry, then the phone rang. It was a friend of her mother's who lived in Ghana, and they laughed and talked for twenty minutes as they planned for her visit to the States. Romi placed her mother's briefcase near the door, and tried not to act as if she were rushing her. She checked the time again.

Her mom hung up the phone, replaced her earring, and checked her hair in the hall mirror. "Romi, are you coming to work with me this evening at the store?" she asked as she picked up her briefcase and headed to the front door. Romi sometimes rode downtown with her dad before he headed to the studio. He'd drop her off at the boutique, and Romi would work a couple of hours, or do her homework in the back room.

"No, Mom. Not tonight." Romi tried to smile and look perfectly natural. "Dad's already gone, and Julio is coming over to . . . to study."

"You were awfully quiet last evening. I thought we might have rented a movie, but it seemed like you just wanted to be alone. Is everything OK? There's no problem with Julio, is there?"

"No, of course not." Romi checked her watch again. "We've just been talking, getting to know each other better. Julio's dad is a little hard to get along with, he says," Romi explained.

"Trouble at home?" Mrs. Cappelle stood at the front door. Her hand was on the knob.

"Not really. Just the usual stuff. It's hard adjusting to a new city."

"I know that must be rough for him. I'm glad he's found you as a friend." Mrs. Cappelle opened the front door and jumped back with a start. Julio stood there, smiling with uncertainty.

"Don't say anything, OK, Mom?" Romi whispered.

"Oh, I wouldn't think of it," her mother whispered back quickly. "Hello again, Julio. Good to see you again."

"Hello, Mrs. Cappelle. Romi is going to help me with my . . ."

"Math!" Romi explained quickly.

"Right, math homework." Julio looked at the ground. He had no book bag, and no book.

Mrs. Cappelle laughed and said, "Right! And I'm the king of Siam! Look, I'm already late. I'm going to go down to the shop, check on the delivery, and help Maisha close up. I should be back by eight."

"Fine, Mom. We'll be here. We might go for a walk or something, but that's all." Romi wished her mother would hurry up and leave.

"You know I trust you, Romi. But you know I'm not real comfortable with just the two of you in the house." She looked Romi straight in the eye.

"I hear you, Mom. We're going to check on the puppies, do our homework, then go for a walk."

"That sounds great. As long as we're on the same page." She kissed her daughter on the cheek. "I'm out of here." She stopped once more. Romi clenched her fists in nervous tension. "Oh, Julio— how's the puppy?"

"Just fine. We named her Taco."

"Cute name. See you kids. Dad's at the station. He doesn't have to do the late news tonight, so he should be home in a couple of hours."

"OK, Mama. See you."

Romi watched her mother's car ease out of the driveway. She breathed a huge sigh of relief. "I was afraid she would never leave," she told Julio. "Ben and Destiny are due here any minute."

Julio tilted his head. "Wait! I hear Ben's car. You can't mistake it."

From the distance they could hear a rumbling, booming sound of bass drums. It got louder as it approached. "What *is* that noise?" Romi asked in disbelief.

Julio laughed. "Ben got his speakers at a garage

sale. They came out of a torn-down movie theater."
The sound was almost deafening as Ben turned the
corner. As he had said, Ben owned the ugliest car in
Cincinnati. It was brown—the color of dirt. The
front bumper was missing, and a huge dent creased
the trunk. Rust dotted the sides like blotches of
disease. It sputtered and coughed and wheezed as it
made its way down the street to Romi's house, but
that noise was overpowered by the sound of the
1812 Overture playing at the loudest possible vol-
ume. Neighbors peeked out of the window to see
what had made such a commotion.

Romi covered her ears. "He's got enough sound
to broadcast at the stadium!"

"That's Ben!" chuckled Julio. "It also covers up the
sound of his bad fan belt and reconditioned engine.
His car stops every other mile."

Destiny got out of the car gingerly, checking to
see that her jacket didn't catch on the coat hanger
that Ben used for a door latch. The sound of sym-
phonies ceased suddenly as Ben turned the motor
off. He jumped out of the other side.

Romi shook with laughter as she watched the
expression on Destiny's face, which was a mixture of
disbelief and exhilaration. Destiny looked at Ben
with awe.

"Do you drive like this all the time, Ben?"

"Sure! I like noise!" he said simply. "Did you
like it?"

"Well, that was an experience I'll never forget!"
Destiny laughed. "Actually, it was live! We'll have to

do that again sometime when my senses recover."
They walked up the steps to Romi's house.

"What's shakin', Destiny?" Romi was still chuckling.

"My ears! I think I used up all the hearing I've got for the next thirty years!" replied Destiny. "But it was pretty awesome too. I could *feel* the drums as they played!"

Ben was pleased. "You got it, Destiny. That's the idea! I can hear and feel every single instrument."

"So could the folks in Spring Grove Cemetery!" added Romi. She let them in the house, and for a moment, each one of them was silent. They just looked at each other, thinking of the dangers that might occur that evening.

Julio spoke first. "Did you bring the camera, Ben?"

"Yep, right here." Ben took a small black box out of his pants pocket. It fit in the palm of his hand. "Just push this button, slip it in your shirt pocket, and forget it. It has a filter that can see through thin material—like shirts—and it picks up any sounds within about one hundred feet."

Romi was impressed. "This is no regular camcorder," she said.

"Of course not," replied Ben. "It was developed for spies in the Middle East. My dad got it from a Japanese dealer of specialty items."

"Wow! A spy camera. Let me see it." Destiny took the small camera and peered through the viewfinder in the back. She saw a perfectly clear picture of Romi's living room, and when she pushed the little red button on the top, she could see extreme close-ups of her friends. She turned the camera to Ben. He noticed she was looking at him, and he grinned. Suddenly embarrassed, she turned the camera on Max, who had slipped in the back door again.

Romi looked doubtful. "Will my dad be able to transfer that to tape?"

"No problem. He can copy it onto a regular-sized tape. It will play on any VCR," Ben reassured her.

Romi sat down on the sofa, and Destiny plopped down beside her. Ben grabbed a chair, but Julio still looked uncomfortable.

"Sit here, Julio," Destiny offered as she scooted to the end of the sofa. "Romi won't mind." Romi smiled, and he finally sat between the two girls, grinning at both of them.

Julio began. "OK, what's the plan? Let's go over this one more time."

"We walk. We talk. We hope they show," Romi said, simplifying the whole matter.

"Then what?" persisted Julio.

"We hope they threaten us like they did yesterday; then we tape them doing it."

Julio continued, "Suppose they want to do more than push us around? They had at least one gun yesterday, and it looked very real."

Destiny responded with determination. "That's where I jump in. I've got my cellular phone, and I double-checked the battery. I can call for help with just one button."

"We'll be right behind you, driving slowly," Ben added.

"In Ben's car. Lord, be with us!" Romi laughed.

"We'll never let you out of our sight. Promise," Ben declared, trying to reassure them.

Julio took a deep breath and looked at Romi. He took her hand in his. "Are you ready?" he asked her.

She squeezed his hand and exhaled. "Let's go," she said, with more bravery than she felt.

39.

Monday—6 P.M.—
The Walk by London Woods

Julio and Romiette walked slowly down the long path that ran past London Woods. Destiny and Ben followed a few yards behind, Ben's car coughing and sputtering but moving steadily. Ben agreed that his music would make him rather noticeable, so all was quiet except for occasional backfires. The weather was cool, and Romi was glad she had brought her jacket. The sky was overcast and gloomy; heavy clouds covered what was left of the sun, and darkness was falling early. Romi shivered, and Julio placed his arm around her shoulder. She moved closer to him. "Are you cold?" he asked her.

"Not anymore," she replied with a smile. He kept his arm loosely around her shoulder as they walked. "Julio, I want to tell you something," Romi began. "I'm really glad we met. Strange things computers do these days."

He grinned and looked at her. "Me too. You have given spice to my life."

"Seems like we have plenty of spice these days— maybe a little too much pepper," Romi joked.

"Or hot sauce?" Julio pretended he had a bottle of hot sauce in his hand and was drinking right from the bottle.

"Yeah, you and your hot sauce!" Romi laughed. "That'll cure those gangbangers!" Then, remembering why they were out there made her suddenly serious. "Julio? Do you think they'll show?"

"Yeah, they'll be here," Julio replied, thinking back angrily to how they had been treated yesterday.

Everything was strangely quiet. Romi and Julio glanced behind them, looking for Ben's car. It sat about two blocks behind them; it had stopped. Ben was looking under the hood, scratching his head, and it looked as if Destiny was pointing out what he should check. She glanced often to check on Julio and Romi as well. They slowed down so as not to get too far ahead.

It was almost dark. The streetlights had clicked on, and the shadows from the trees made Sunday's afternoon walk in the sunlight seem quite pleasant. Julio grabbed Romi's hand again. The same electricity that she had felt the very first time he held her hand buzzed through her like lightning once more. He felt it too. He glanced at her face—her eyes, which were honey brown, and her nose, which crinkled when she smiled. He touched the soft brown tendrils of hair that curled and circled her face. She sighed slowly. She said nothing, but her eyes never left his.

Julio glanced toward a small dirt path that led from the walkway into the woods. He whispered, "Romi—look. Let's check out that tree over there."

She looked to where he was pointing. "Julio, there are a million trees in the distance. Can you be more specific?"

"That one"—he smiled—"the one with the brown trunk and the skinny branches."

"Oh, sure, that one." Romi was perplexed. Why was he so interested in trees all of a sudden? She wanted to grow roots right there on that sidewalk and never leave that spot. Still holding her hand, Julio pulled her gently toward the narrow trail.

"This one. Right here down this little path. Look, Romi. You have to see this."

She tried to peer through the dark woods. "What is it?" she asked. But she didn't protest as Julio led her about two yards down the trail. Romi shivered again, not from fear, and not from cold, but from the closeness of Julio in the darkness. "If we leave the road, Ben and Destiny can't see us," she said weakly.

"If we leave the road, Ben and Destiny can't see me kiss you," Julio replied softly as he pulled her close to him. She inhaled slowly. His lips touched hers lightly, then the kiss became a flower that blossomed and bloomed in the darkness.

"Oh, Julio," was all Romi could say. He murmured her name as he held her. All his anger, fear, and frustration melted on that dark evening as he held Romiette in his arms. She had never felt so alive, so aware of the sounds of the branches swaying in the chilly wind, of the smell of the damp earth below them.

He touched her face with his fingers, traced her lips

with his fingertips. She could tell he was smiling in the darkness. "Yep, it was hot sauce," he teased her. "Right there on your lips. I had to get it off, you know."

"That was lipstick," she teased back.

"Hot sauce," he said slowly.

"Lipstick," she protested weakly.

His lips searched for hers once more in the darkness. They forgot about their problems, the gang, even Ben and Destiny, who now seemed so far away. They were only aware of each other, of the bright and sparkling warmth of that moment, of the fresh new joy of that kiss.

"You are my hot sauce," he whispered in her ear.

"I love the way you say things," she whispered in return. Romi wanted that moment to last forever, but she knew they'd better head back. "Let's get back on the road," she said reluctantly. "We don't want Ben and Destiny to get worried. Hold my hand." Julio held her hand tightly as he led her back to the sidewalk.

"Do you see them?" Romi asked. Very little light remained in the sky. It would be night soon, and the darkening clouds and increasing winds indicated a storm was on its way. Romi, though, felt safe and warm—the whole world glowed in spite of the oncoming storm and night.

Julio peered into the darkness. "Yeah, I see them. They're *pushing* the car!"

"A lot of good they are for protection! I can't wait to hear Destiny complain about this one! Should we go help them?"

"No," Julio answered. "They're doing just fine. They'll be here in a few minutes. So that gives us time for just one more taste of hot sauce!" He grabbed her waist and quickly kissed her once more. They gazed at each other in the light of the street lamp and grinned.

The moment was shattered suddenly by the blast of a car horn. Julio and Romi jumped with surprise and moved very close together. It wasn't Ben's car that pulled up next to them, however; it was the black Cadillac of the Devildog gang. It approached from the north, spun around, did a sharp U-turn, and rolled smoothly to a stop directly in front of them. The car had never even passed Ben and Destiny. Romi's heart, which was still fluttering from Julio's touch, began to pound. Julio, determined to protect Romi at all costs, planted his feet firmly on the sidewalk and angrily awaited the approach of the gang members. He reached into his front shirt pocket and clicked the video camera on. All was silent. There was no sign of Ben and Destiny.

"Stay calm and relaxed," he whispered to Romi. "Make them talk. The more they say, the more we have to use against them."

"Where are Ben and Destiny?" Romi worried. "Shouldn't they be here by now? Suppose they don't get here in time?"

"Relax." Julio's voice was soothing and soft. "They'll get here. They've got the phone to call for help."

The doors of the Cadillac opened, and as before, the four boys got out in unison. They looked serious and threatening in the dim light of the street lamp. The last to step out of the car was Malaka. Romi gasped. Malaka took her place next to Terrell.

Terrell spoke. "Romiette," he said in a lazy, gravelly voice, "I thought we had you schooled. What's up with this Tex-Mex boy? Why you still hangin' with him?"

"I told you, Terrell, I will not be intimidated by you, or the Devildogs, or anybody else!" Romi was so angry, she was close to tears. Julio stood protectively next to her. "And Malaka, what are you doing here? You're going to be sorry you got involved in this. You're way out of your league, girlfriend."

Malaka replied viciously, "No, honey. *You* the one who's gonna be sorry. This *is* my league!"

Terrell smiled and put his arm around her. He looked relaxed and in control. "The Devildogs rule, and you gotta learn that."

Julio took a step forward. "Look, Terrell, why don't you and the Devildogs just leave Romi and me alone. We won't bother you and we won't report you to the cops."

Terrell spat on the ground. "What cops?" he replied with derision. "What they gonna do to us? Devildogs rule, Tex. And we 'bout to show you how. We tried to warn you, but you got to be taught a lesson."

"What do you plan to do?" Romi asked, fear making her voice quaver a bit.

Terrell was pleased to hear the fear, and he knew that Julio, although tough, was helpless in the face of a gun. He barked his commands quickly. "Rashad,

Mookie, Iceman—the plan. Do it! Malaka, get in the car." She obeyed.

Instantly the three young men moved forward. Two grabbed Julio before he could react. He fought and cursed and struggled, then he felt the cold steel of a gun on his neck. He stood very still as they tied his arms. The one called Rashad grabbed Romi and roughly yanked her arms behind her. She screamed, "Get your hands off me! Julio! Help!" Her screams were muffled and silenced suddenly as Terrell tossed a dirty sweatshirt over her head. She gasped in confusion and terror as she felt herself being picked up and carried by two sets of arms.

Julio tried to twist toward her, but the barrel of the gun pushed deeper into his neck. He was frantic and kicked his strong legs at his attackers. Terrell, however, moved behind Julio and struck him just behind his knees. Julio fell forward onto his face, but continued to fight. He butted Mookie with his head and rolled over so that his legs kicked Iceman in the shin. "Romi!" Julio yelled. "I won't let them—" At that, he felt a sickening thud as the butt of the gun hit the back of his head. Julio faced the sky, but darkness had taken him, and the videotape had recorded it all.

The whole ordeal took less than three minutes. Terrell looked around and saw two figures pushing a car in the distance. "Hurry up!" he yelled at his gang. "Get them in the car before somebody comes! Let's get out of here!"

40.

The Six O'clock Evening News—Monday

—Good evening. It's six o'clock on Channel Six, and this is the news. I am Cornell Cappelle, and with me is Nannette Norris. Good evening, Nannette.

—Hello, Cornell. In the news tonight, the Reds get a new stadium, the Bengals get a new stadium, and plans are being made to get the Olympics to come to Cincinnati in the year 2016. The Olympics? Gee, what a hassle that would be. All those people, and the traffic!

—Thank you, Nannette. I think we have several years before we have to worry about that reality. Perhaps by then you will have made it to prime-time news and moved to New York.

—Oh, no, Cornell. I couldn't possibly leave the TV Six news team. What would you do without me?

—I don't know, Nannette. Life around here certainly would not be the same! Also tonight we will continue our special report on teenage gangs in our cities. TV Six has been investigating this story for some time, and it seems that the threat may be overrated. Although our schools have some problems with guns and teen-related crimes, we have found no real evidence of the existence of established gangs in our city. Our children do not have the same pressures as students in Los Angeles or New

York, for example, and we are fortunate to be able to handle these problems in the schools through normal channels of discipline. We will continue this report as our investigation continues. Back to you, Nannette.

—*We'll be back in a moment with exclusive footage of a deer stuck on I-75. Details in a moment.*

—*Struck, Nannette, not stuck. A car hit a deer on the road.*

—*And then the deer stuck to the highway?*

—*Let's pause here for a station break. We'll be right back.*

41.

The Cappelle Home—
Monday—9 P.M.

Mrs. Cappelle had had a terrible day. She got to work late, the shipment was wrong and had to be reprocessed, a customer came in and stayed for two hours, trying on dozens of outfits, then ended up buying only a hair clip on sale for fifty cents. She finally eased into her car and headed home. She hoped Romi had cooked something. She was starving. She pulled into the driveway just ahead of her husband, who had come home early too since he didn't have to do the eleven o'clock broadcast. They pulled both cars into the garage and stood together for a moment looking at the threatening sky. The air smelled of rain. Cornell Cappelle breathed deeply of the fresh night air. He held his wife's hand and sighed. "You know, Lady B., I love my job, and I'm good at it. But that Nannette is going to drive me to drink! She is a total idiot!"

She loved when he called her Lady B. It had been his pet name for her when they were dating in college. "How much longer can they keep her on?" she asked.

"Who knows?" he replied with consternation. "Her uncle is somebody who works in management upstairs."

"Ratings down at all?" his wife asked as they opened the front door.

"I think ratings are going up because people are watching the show just to laugh at her. It's not a comedy show—it's supposed to be the news!" Cornell responded angrily.

She tried to soothe him a bit and change the subject. "Something's got to give soon, dear. Are you hungry?"

"Yeah, starving. Let's order Chinese. Where's Romi?"

"Sounds good to me. Probably in her room. Romi! We're going to order Chinese food. Want some?" Mrs. Cappelle called. She heard only silence.

"That's odd," remarked Mr. Cappelle. "Maybe she's out back with the dogs." He strode through the kitchen and looked out the back door. "ROMI!" he called loudly.

"I don't think she's here, Cornell." Fear edged Mrs. Cappelle's voice. They checked all the rooms in the house and found only darkness and silence.

"Let's check the answering machine and see if she's left a message," Cornell suggested. They did, but all they heard were messages from salespeople and business associates.

"It's after dark, and she hasn't called. This is not like her." He sat on the sofa, a frown on his face. "Well, where could she be? Destiny's house?"

"I don't think so, Cornell. When I left for work, she was studying math with the young man from school she gave the puppy to. His name is Julio—Hispanic kid—nice-looking. I think she likes him. I've never seen her grin so much."

"You left her here with a boy you don't know?" Mr. Cappelle asked his wife accusingly, worry in his voice.

She responded, "It was bright daylight, and they were doing homework. I trust her. She probably just lost track of the time, Cornell. You know how it is."

"Well, Miss Romiette and Mr. Julio had better call soon. She is usually a lot more responsible. I don't like this, and I'm getting really worried." Cornell Cappelle walked across the living-room floor several times. On the floor next to the coffee table was a small square of paper. He recognized Romi's handwriting and picked it up quickly. "Lady B.! Here's a note that Romi left. It must have blown to the floor." They read it together.

> Mom,
> I went for a walk with Julio.
> I'll be back by seven.
> Love, Romi

"Seven?" Mrs. Cappelle said in alarm. "It's almost ten o'clock, Cornell."

"Did she leave a number?" Cornell asked. "Do you know his last name?"

"No, he's new. Just moved here a couple of months

ago. I know she talks to him quite a bit on the phone, and she told me that she first met him on the Internet."

"Internet? That's how criminals find innocent young girls and then seduce and attack them. What do you know about this kid?" stormed Cornell.

His wife said calmly, "He certainly didn't look like a criminal. He was personable, polite, and downright cute. I think he liked her too."

"Now I'm really worried," Cornell said. "We did a story on Internet criminals. If he's so sweet and innocent, where is she?"

"Now, let's not jump to conclusions. Let me call Destiny's house." Romi's mother picked up the phone and called the familiar number. "Hello, Janell, how are you?"

"Working hard, Brianna, as usual. Are the girls at your house?"

Romi's mother caught her breath. "No, Janell, that's why I called. You haven't seen them?"

"No, not today. Destiny left shortly after she got home from school with a boy named Ben. Cute kid with blue hair. She said they were going to the library to do some research. The library closes at nine, so she should be home soon."

"Blue hair?" Mrs. Cappelle questioned.

"Yes, bright blue. And pierced ears, and nose, and eyebrow." Destiny's mother sighed. "But Destiny says he makes straight A's. Kids these days."

"Well, would you call me the instant she comes in? I don't know where Romiette is, and I'm a little worried. I'm sure it's nothing, but when they start driving, and riding with kids with blue hair, I worry."

"Sure, Brianna. I'll have her call you. And you let me know if Romi gets there before we call."

"Thanks, Janell. I'll talk to you soon." Mrs. Cappelle hung up the phone and frowned. A heavy feeling of dread slowly crept into her body. Something was not right.

Cornell felt it too. "Who else can we call, Lady?" He was pacing the floor.

"It's a long shot, but let me call her friend Malaka Grimes. They used to be close, and I know they talked just recently about some activity at school. Let's see, her number is here on the refrigerator somewhere. Here it is." She punched the number quickly. Her fingers were beginning to shake. "Hello, Malaka, this is Mrs. Cappelle. Have you seen Romi?"

Malaka was in a hurry, but when she heard Romi's mother's voice, her breath caught in her throat. She had only stopped by her house to get some duct tape that Rashad had forgotten. She wished she hadn't answered the phone. Outside, in front of her house, Terrell and the Devildogs waited impatiently. They had important business tonight, and Romi's mother was the last person Malaka felt like talking to. She answered quickly, "I don't talk to her much anymore since she started hanging with that foreigner."

"Foreigner?"

"Yeah, that new kid. I think he's trouble."

"Why?" The chill of dread was spreading quickly through Mrs. Cappelle's body.

Malaka felt powerful. She added maliciously, "I think he's got gang connections. That's why they moved here, I heard."

"Do you know this for a fact, or are you going by hearsay?"

"I just know what I know," Malaka replied sullenly. "Hey, I gotta go."

Romi's mother could feel Malaka's negative attitude. She knew she'd get very little further information. "Thanks, Malaka," she said politely. "If you hear from her, call me, OK? I'm getting really worried." Mrs. Cappelle could hear a car horn honking furiously in the background, but she thought nothing of it.

"Sure," Malaka replied shortly. "Bye." She hung up and grinned. *Terrell would be proud of me,* she told herself as she bounded down the stairs and out to the Devildogs.

Mrs. Cappelle hung the phone up slowly. "That was odd," she said to her husband. "Malaka said the new kid was trouble."

Cornell turned and faced his wife with anger and worry. "See, I told you! I'm calling the police!"

His wife handed him the phone. "You're right," she said, shaking. "I hope we're overreacting, but let's call." Mr. Cappelle's mind was numb. He couldn't believe he was about to call the police about his precious daughter, his Romiette, his princess. Then the doorbell rang, jarring his thoughts.

He walked to the front door and looked out the small glass window. Two police officers in blue stood on his doorstep. Behind them stood Destiny and a boy he had never seen before, the kid with the blue hair. His heart pounded with dread. He looked back at his wife, whose eyes were wide with fright. "It's the police," he said quietly. She gasped. He opened the front door, hoping for a miracle, but fearing the worst.

"Mr. and Mrs. Cappelle?" the officer asked.

"Yes, please come in. Does this have something to do with our daughter? What's happened?"

Mrs. Cappelle gulped huge breaths of air. She fought back tears. "Oh, my God! Destiny? Why are you with the police? Where's Romi? What's going on? Who's the boy with the blue hair?" She was getting frantic.

The police officer, who had encountered many distraught parents, took control of the situation. He spoke calmly and quietly. "Let's start at the beginning, ma'am. May I sit down?"

"Yes, please." She motioned vaguely toward the sofa. She sat on the edge of a chair, every fiber bristling with concern. Cornell did not sit. He continued to pace while he listened.

The police officer continued. "At 7:12 P.M. this evening a 911 call came into dispatch, apparently from Miss Dodson here and Mr. Olsen. They had called to report that their friends, your daughter, Romiette, and a young man by the name of Julio Montague, were apparently missing."

"Missing?" Romi's mother stood up. "What do you mean, *missing?* And why did you say 'apparently' missing?"

Destiny went over to Romi's mother and took her cold and shaking hand. Destiny's hands were cold as well. "Mrs. C., let me tell you the whole story. I'm so scared. It wasn't supposed to happen this way."

"OK, Destiny, let's sit down. Now tell me everything. Start at the beginning. Young man, are you part of this?"

"Yes, ma'am. My name is Ben. We had a plan, but then something went wrong, and I'm really sorry. Romi never was sure about this whole idea. And Julio said we ought to tell . . ." Ben looked down at the floor in shame and confusion.

"Tell what?" Cornell demanded. "Will somebody please explain what's going on? We don't know where my daughter is, and I want to get to the bottom of this now! Destiny, you start."

She took a deep breath. "OK. It all started with the Scientific Soul Mate System."

"The what?"

"No, wait, that's stupid. That was just a game. This is real. It all started when Romiette and Julio started talking on the Internet. Most of the time the kids we talk to in the chat rooms live in other cities, other states, but it turned out that Romi and Julio lived right here in Cincinnati, and even went to the same school. Freaky."

"I told you about Internet criminals!" Cornell declared angrily.

"Let her finish, Cornell. Go on, Destiny." One police officer took notes. The other stood by the door and watched the scene silently.

Destiny started to cry. "Ben, you go on. I'm shaking too hard to talk."

"Julio is no criminal, Mr. C. Romiette and Julio got to talking at school and they kinda liked each other. Julio told me he was lonely and missed his friends at his old school and Romiette was his first real friend here. And me and Julio really hit it off right away." Ben touched his nose instinctively. "I guess he liked my style."

"Blue hair, right?" Mrs. Cappelle smiled in spite of herself.

"Sometimes it's green. Last week it was orange."

"Get on with the story, Ben," Mr. Cappelle urged.

"OK. Julio and Romi have been getting hassled at school by these kids that are in the Devildogs."

"Devildogs?"

"Yeah, this gang at school."

"What gang? What's this about a gang?" Cornell asked.

"There's lots of gangs around here. In our city. In our school. Your news reports are wrong, Mr. Cappelle. You want to know the real deal? Why don't you ask the kids?"

"You're right, Ben. We'll do that. But go on—tell us how all this fits into the story. Where is Romiette?" He wanted to pull his hair out. This seemed to be going so slowly, and Romiette was not sitting in her living room where she was supposed to be.

"Well, I got this Minicam from my dad—it's like a spy recorder or something—and the plan was that we would secretly tape the Devildogs threatening

Julio and Romiette. Then we were going to turn the tape over to you, Mr. Cappelle, so you could expose them on TV, and that would be the end of that."

"But that's so dangerous! What possessed you kids to undertake something so potentially life-threatening?" Cornell was furious.

"Julio wants to be a news cameraman or something. Plus he wanted to show Romi he was brave and would protect her. We figured we could handle it." The answer sounded stupid to Ben even as he said it.

Destiny tried to help him. "See, Ben and me were supposed to follow behind in his car with a cell phone. And we could call if anything got out of hand."

"But my car stopped, and we tried to push it, but cars are a lot heavier than they look! By the time we got it started, and we got to the place where Romi and Julio were supposed to be, they were gone!"

"What do you mean *gone?*"

"They were only about a block or so ahead of us—walking on the sidewalk that goes past London Woods. We knew they wouldn't go into the woods because it was getting dark, and we had already talked about that. The plan was to stay where we could see them so nobody could get hurt."

Destiny couldn't stop crying. "We looked in the woods anyway and we called and yelled. But they just weren't there!" She buried her face in her hands and sobbed.

Ben added, "That's when we called 911. The police officers came, but they didn't really believe us at first.

It does sound a little suspicious. 'Our friends are not where they said they would be' doesn't sound like a serious problem, but we were really worried.'"

Destiny took the tissue Mrs. Cappelle offered and wiped her eyes and nose. "I'm scared, Mrs. C. Something really bad has happened. Romi wouldn't run off like this, and they're not in the woods, and the Devildogs have been threatening them. . . ."

Cornell Cappelle looked directly at the two policemen. "Officers, what do we do now? I want my daughter found!"

"We are starting a full investigation, sir. We will search London Woods and the surrounding areas. Did you kids see any unusual cars or vehicles?"

"No. Nothing. The street was deserted. Just us and the breeze," Ben said quietly.

"I'm scared, Mrs. C.," Destiny said again. "I always play around and tell people that I'm psychic, but something tells me something really bad has happened. What are we gonna do?"

"I'll kill that kid if he's hurt my daughter!"

Destiny looked surprised. "Julio wouldn't hurt Romi, Mr. C. He's crazy about her!"

"Oh, Cornell, what are we going to do?" Mrs. Cappelle went over to her husband and buried her face in his frightened embrace.

"Let's not throw words like 'kill' around, folks," admonished the policeman with the notepad. "Hold on, I've got a call here from dispatch." He put his walkie-talkie to his ear. "Yeah, Joe? OK. We'll be right down with the parents of the girl." He looked at Romi's parents. "Mr. and Mrs. Cappelle, Julio's parents are on their way to the station. They called a few minutes ago to report their son hadn't come home from school. Ordinarily we wouldn't worry much about a teenager coming home late from school. But this is different. It seems that your daughter and their son are missing together."

Romi's parents held on to each other for a moment, then they hurriedly gathered their things to head to the police station. Mrs. Cappelle looked at Destiny. "Destiny, call your mother right away, and tell her everything. Then go home and stay there. If Romi tries to contact anybody, she'll call you if she can't reach us. We'll call you later and let you know what's going on. Make sure the door is locked when you leave." Destiny nodded, still sniffing. "Ben, will your car get her home safely?"

"Yes, ma'am. Turns out it was out of gas. I'll take her home. And Mrs. Cappelle—I'm really sorry."

"I know, Ben. Let's just hope this turns out to be less than what we fear. Good night." She turned then and walked into the night with the police officers. It had started to rain.

42.

In the Montague Car—
9:30 P.M.

Luis Montague was angry—and afraid. He gripped the steering wheel fiercely and looked straight ahead as he drove to the police station. His wife sat beside him, weeping. They did not speak. The windshield wipers squeaked back and forth as the rain pelted the car.

His thoughts exploded finally. "I told him to leave that girl alone!" he yelled to the sky, to the rain, to his wife. "I warned him about hanging around with those people!"

"Luis, we're not sure about anything yet. Please don't jump to conclusions."

"Don't tell me how to think!" he roared. Then, softer, he said, "I'm sorry, Maria. I'm just so worried. I can't believe we're heading to the police station because our son is missing."

"Maybe he's got a good excuse. Maybe we're overreacting," she offered, searching for hope. "Are we being foolish?"

"We've been over this, Maria. Something is wrong. You were home all day, right?"

"Yes."

"And Julio didn't come home from school."

"Maybe he had band practice or something," Maria suggested weakly.

"From three o'clock until ten? Not likely. And he hasn't called?"

"No," she admitted. "And that's not like him at all."

"And did we try to call his friends, what few we know of?" he demanded, trying to make himself understand this terror as well.

"Well, we called that young man, Ben, whom he seems to be quite close to, and there was no answer. And we have called the school, and gone down to the school building to find it locked and dark."

"So what choice do we have, Maria?" Luis asked in resignation. "The boy loves that puppy and wouldn't leave it for hours unattended like this. And he knows how you worry about him. He would not do this to his mother. I know my son. Something is wrong."

"But what makes you think it has something to do with this girl, Luis? I know he really likes her. I could see the glow in his smile when he spoke of her. We had a good talk about his feelings for her."

"I told him not to get involved with gang kids like that! How dare you encourage him?" Luis asked, his anger returning.

Julio's mother retorted, "If you wouldn't yell at him and threaten him, Luis, he might confide in you more!" Luis refused to answer. Maria continued, "And what makes you think she's involved in a gang?

He would have told me if he even suspected that. He's been through the pain of gangs back home. He wouldn't voluntarily jump into those muddy waters again."

"That's not what he told me. He defied me and dared me to try to run his life!"

"Perhaps Julio is right, Luis," his wife said quietly.

"What?"

"Perhaps you should let him make his own decisions, and his own mistakes, just as we did." She waited for her husband's stormy reaction. But he was quiet and thoughtful.

"Perhaps so," he finally said sadly, "but none of this answers the question I want to know most. Where is my son? Where is Julio?"

They pulled into the parking lot of the police station. They got out in the pouring rain and, sharing one umbrella, hurried inside.

43.

At the Station—10 P.M.

The inside of the police station didn't look anything like the police stations she had seen on TV, Mrs. Montague thought. It had a very small, dimly lit waiting room. The police officer behind the bullet-proof glass window looked bored and unconcerned when they walked in out of the rain.

"Excuse me, sir," began Luis. The words were difficult for him to say. The thought that something might have happened to Julio made the words stick in his mouth. "We wish . . . we wish to report our son is missing. I called earlier and I was asked to come down here."

"How old is he?" the officer asked.

"Sixteen," Mrs. Montague answered.

"How long has he been gone?"

"He didn't come home from school today, and he has not called. That is not like my son," she said with assurance.

"Did you have a fight? Is there any reason why he would run away?" Seeing the pained looked on Maria Montague's face, he added gently, "I'm sorry, folks. These are routine questions. We need all the information we can get in order to find your son."

"I understand," replied Mrs. Montague with dignity. "There has been no fight; well, some minor disagreements, maybe, but my Julio would not run away."

The officer looked up. "Did you say 'Julio'? What's his full name?"

"Julio Leonardo Montague," his father replied. The officer checked a dispatch paper in front of him. "Would you folks have a seat for just a minute? We had a 911 call earlier today from some kids who mentioned your son's name. Our captain is on his way here now, and he told me he wanted to speak with you personally."

Fearing the worst, Mrs. Montague began to weep again. She collapsed in her husband's arms. "Perhaps he has good news, Maria," Luis said to her as he tried to comfort her. But he didn't believe it himself. He too swallowed dread as he waited for the captain to return.

The rain and wind blew harder. The Montagues listened to the rain on the windows as they waited.

Finally, the door blew open, and two police officers and an African-American couple walked in the door. Maria recognized the man right away. He was Cornell Cappelle, the good-looking newsman from Channel Six. She whispered to her husband, "I think those are the parents of the girl."

Luis also recognized Cappelle. But he showed no sign of acknowledgment or recognition. The mother had been crying, he could tell, and the father looked as fierce and frightened as Luis himself felt.

The captain checked in at the dispatch desk and glanced over at the Montagues after a word with the officer behind the window. He smiled, and walked over with confidence, his hand outstretched. "Mr. and Mrs. Montague? I'm Bill Escaluski, captain here."

"Glad to meet you, sir. Do you know anything about my son?" Mrs. Montague wanted to skip the polite nonessentials.

"Not yet, but we're working on it. Let me introduce you to the other half of this puzzle." Romi's mother and father walked over to Julio's mother and father. "Mr. and Mrs. Cappelle," he said, "meet Mr. and Mrs. Montague. That's funny—the Montagues and the Cappelles. I remember those names from high school, or something very close to it—Shakespeare. Enemies, weren't they? In *Romeo and Juliet*. Even your kids' names are similar."

Cornell Cappelle was in no mood for humorous coincidences. "We don't find anything very funny about this evening." He looked at Luis Montague with distrust. "If your boy has hurt my child in any way, I swear, I'll—"

Luis was about to respond angrily, when the captain interrupted. "Right now, folks, we have no proof that anyone has done anything wrong. Both young people may be in grave danger. Let's see if we can get to the bottom of this together."

Lady Brianna Cappelle smiled at Maria Montague and offered her hand. Then she said to her husband,

"Cornell, calm down. There's got to be a logical explanation for all this. I'm sure that the Montagues are just as worried as we are."

Maria returned her smile. "Thank you, Mrs. Cappelle. Julio is a good boy, a quiet, studious boy who likes music and computers. He would not hurt anyone. My husband is afraid that perhaps by befriending your daughter, his life may have been put in danger."

"Danger? How? And why, because of our daughter?" Cornell Cappelle bristled at the accusation.

"He hinted to me that he had been threatened at school because of his ethnic heritage and because of his friendship with your daughter. I wish I had paid more attention. As his father, I worry, of course. You understand, don't you?"

"So there has been trouble at school and at home, am I right, folks?" interjected the captain.

"Not enough for both of them to disappear like this," retorted Luis. "We left Texas because of this kind of trouble—gangs and such."

"What kind of trouble, Mr. Montague? What do you mean—gangs?" Cornell asked with defiance. "I heard it was *your* son who was the troublemaker!"

"Quite the contrary," retorted Luis. "It was gangs. They ruled the schools there. We left Texas to get a new start for our son, a chance for him to grow up independent and safe."

"Was he in a gang? Is that why there's trouble now?" Mrs. Cappelle asked.

"No, we think it is your daughter who might be

involved in a gang here. That is why there is trouble. I have seen this before. The girlfriends of the gang boys often help them to target the boys." Luis refused to budge from his belief. It was the only way he could face this ordeal.

"Nonsense! Romi would never do something like that! And there's no way she is involved in any gang! She doesn't even have a boyfriend. And she certainly would not stoop to target your son for another boy to hurt. How dare you!" Cornell was angry enough to fight.

Mrs. Montague said gently as she touched Cornell's arm, "We too are hurt when you suggest that my son is involved in the disappearance of your daughter. We are very worried that he might be hurt . . . or worse."

Cornell took her hand in his and exhaled. "I'm sorry. I apologize. Let's start over, and see if we can get to the bottom of this." Both mothers smiled and sighed with relief.

Captain Escaluski pulled up a folding chair and sat between the two families. He thought out loud, "Suppose the problem is not that Romi or Julio are involved in a gang, but that they were both targeted by a gang?"

Luis responded, "For what reason? Julio is new here—we've only been here in Cincinnati a few months. Romiette was his first real friend."

Mrs. Cappelle shook her head. "I think it might be a little more than friendship. I saw them looking at each other this afternoon. There was more than friendship in the looks they gave each other." She smiled sadly, remembering.

The captain made note of this and asked, "Do you think they ran away together? Is that a possibility? Maybe they felt threatened and decided to run away from all their problems. Believe me, I've seen it happen hundreds of times. And the parents never want to admit it's a possibility."

"My Julio would not run away," murmured Maria Montague quietly.

"And I don't think Romi would either, but maybe we don't know the whole story," admitted Romi's mother.

"From what Destiny and Ben told us, the kids had some kind of crazy plan to videotape the gang members threatening them. That doesn't sound like a runaway plot—it sounds to me like their plan went very wrong," reasoned Cornell. "And we are wasting time here. We've got to find them!"

The captain agreed. "OK. We know that Julio had a hidden camera that he was going to use to catch the gang members and expose them. He wanted to stop the gang from threatening Romi. And we know that Ben and Destiny were supposed to be following in Ben's car, and in the time that it took to get Ben's car started again, Romiette and Julio disappeared. Right now, we know nothing for sure about a gang. On the information we have, I'm organizing my men for a full search. Let's get busy."

Cornell checked his watch. "Lady B., I'm going to run down to the station. If I hurry, I can get it at the beginning of the broadcast for the eleven o'clock news. Maybe somebody out there saw something."

"Good idea, Cornell. Please be careful. That storm is terrible."

"I'll pick you up after the show. Will you be all right?" he asked, touching the tears on her face.

"I'm not leaving this place until I hear some good news about my baby," she said with determination. He smiled, kissed her on the cheek, and hurried outside into the storm. He needed action, and this was something he knew he could do.

"Oh, God, where are they?" Julio's mother began to weep again. Romi's mother held her hand. The thunder outside exploded deafeningly as the rain pelted the window of the police station waiting room.

44.

The Eleven O'clock Evening News

MISSING—ROMIETTE CAPPELLE AND JULIO MONTAGUE. Details in a moment.

—In this modern-day, mystery version of Romeo and Juliet, two young people have vanished. We ask for the help of the public. If anyone has any knowledge of these two young people, last seen walking past London Woods between six and seven this evening, please call District Four police. Romiette Cappelle is the daughter of our own Cornell Cappelle. Cornell, I know this is difficult, but a few words, please.

—"If you have my daughter, or know where she is, or know anything about where she and Julio Montague might be, please call the station. She's sixteen years old, and the light of my life. Please. Please."

—Pictures of the two young people will be posted throughout the city. There is a five-thousand-dollar reward for any information leading to the recovery of Romiette and Julio. Romiette is sixteen years old, five feet five inches, with brown skin and hazel eyes. Julio is also sixteen, is about six feet tall, and has curly black hair.

—TV Six has been investigating the increase of gang activity in our schools and our city. After further investigation, we find that reports *of gang fights in the high schools and gang recruitment at the junior high level has been discovered. Much of the increased gun violence has been attributed to gang activity. The mayor has appointed a task force to study the matter. News Six will continue to investigate.*

—In the weather tonight, our TV Six meteorologists warn of heavy rain, and maybe even thunderstorms, unusual for this time of the year, heading this way. Not good for two kids who may be in the woods lost or hurt. Details when we return from station break.

45.

Romi's Parents at Home—
Midnight

The Cappelles sat huddled together in their dark-
ened living room. The storm raged outside, and their
fears raged inside. Cornell had picked his wife up
from the station after the newscast, and even though
she didn't want to leave, he had convinced her that
nothing more could be done there tonight. She kept
glancing at the telephone, willing it to ring. "Oh,
Cornell, I can't bear it. It's so long. I will never sleep,
never rest, never breathe right again until Romi
comes bouncing through that door." She let herself
sob uncontrollably now.

"Where could they be?" he mused. "I know Romi
would have called if she were . . . OK. Do you think
she saw my news report?"

"If she had seen it, she would have called," her
mother answered sadly.

"I still think that kid had something to do with all
this," muttered Romi's father. "If she hadn't been
with him, none of this would have happened. This
is your fault, Lady. You shouldn't have let her go
running off with some kid she didn't even know.

You shouldn't have left her here alone with him!"

She bristled in response. "Now, don't you even start that stuff with me. I know you're upset, and you know that nobody could have foreseen how a study date could turn into such tragedy."

"I know, Lady, I'm sorry. I just want to scream! Let's go looking for her. We can't just sit here, waiting for them to tell us they found her body!"

"Sh-sh-sh. They're gonna find our baby. And she's gonna be just fine. I have to believe it. I just have to. We've gotta wait here in case they call."

"Do you think that boy is an innocent victim too, Lady?"

"I believe the Montague family. I don't think he'd hurt her. I think he might have been in love with her, Cornell," she said with a slight smile.

"Love?" he scoffed. "What does a sixteen-year-old know about love?"

"That's how old I was when I fell in love with you, Cornell," she reminded him quietly.

"OK, OK, you're right. But this is my baby girl we're talking about. She was the light of my life. You know that, Lady."

"She still *is* your light and bright star-child, Cornell. Quit talking in the past tense! We're going to find them. Both of them."

The storm continued, loud and furious. The Cappelles sat silently and waited.

46.

Julio's Parents at Home—
2 A.M.

The Montagues sat at their kitchen table, watching the storm and, like the Cappelles, waiting for the phone to ring. Maria had made a pot of coffee, and they sipped it quietly, wishing and praying that this night would disappear. The puppy slept by their feet.

"Remember when Julio was a baby," she said, "and he was so afraid of thunderstorms?"

Luis smiled. "And then he grew up, determined not to be afraid of anything!" He sighed. "I am afraid, tonight, Maria. Terrified."

"I am too. I can't even bear to pause at all the terrible things my mind makes me think." She wept quietly.

"Did we do wrong, Maria, to bring him here away from his friends and relatives?" Luis asked.

"No, Luis. We agreed it was best. Even Julio was glad to get away from that environment, even though it was hard for him to leave his friends at school. A boy should not have to fight his way through high school just to survive. We made the right choice."

"But it seems the fight followed him here in spite of us."

"Julio is strong—in his body as well as in his heart and mind. He will come out of this victorious and even stronger. You will see." Maria believed in her son.

The phone rang, jangling the silence between Maria and Luis. His hands and voice shaking, Luis picked up the receiver. His wife could tell nothing from the expression on his face, which was impassive. He only said, "Yes, yes. We'll be right down!" He hung up the phone.

"Did they find Julio?" his wife entreated.

"No, but they picked up some kids for speeding. Their car tires match the tire tracks in the park, and they've arrested the kids in it."

"Kids? Whose car is it?"

"It was being driven by a boy from their school. Five teenagers, four boys and a girl, were in the car— all dressed in purple, and all carrying guns." He paused angrily as he put his coat on. "Sounds like a gang to me! Let's go."

The Montagues arrived at the police station just before the Cappelles. Captain Escaluski met them at the door. "We are taking you to view the young people we arrested. We just want to know if you recognize any of them," he told the four parents. He led them down a dim hall and into a large room. One wall was a window. Mrs. Montague clutched her husband's hand in fear. "They can't see you behind this glass window. Do you recognize any of them?"

Mrs. Cappelle gasped. "Oh, my—yes! That's Malaka, Romi's friend, or at least she used to be. I called her when I got home from work; that's when I was looking for Romi and couldn't find her. She sounded a little—strange."

"Strange?"

"Yes." Mrs. Cappelle paused, trying to remember. "I know she was in a big hurry, and she was very negative about Romi's relationship with Julio—she called him a foreigner. I don't know, but I have a feeling she knows something."

"Joe, bring her out—I want to talk to her," the captain ordered. "Do you recognize any of the others, folks?"

"No, those are not the kinds of kids Romi hangs out with. These are hard-looking, angry young men. Romi would have stayed away from them."

"My Julio as well," said his mother.

"Are you sure?" the captain insisted. "Kids change, you know, and sometimes parents are the last to know about their children's activities."

"What do you mean, 'parents are the last to know'? You saying I don't know my daughter? You saying my daughter is mixed up with these gang kids? I ought to . . ." Cornell's anger was getting the best of him again.

"Cornell, calm down," his wife soothed. "He's just trying to cover all his bases. Officer, you must understand. Our daughter is *not* a part of these young people. She's home with her family most of the time, she

works at my shop with me in her spare time, she's a
fine athlete, and she makes good grades in school.
I've met most of her friends because they feel comfortable hanging out at our home. She doesn't even
date much. If she's involved with these young people that you say are connected to a gang, then somehow, for some reason, she has been targeted by them.
But understand this clearly, she is *not* a part of them."

"I hear you, ma'am. But it is my job to investigate.
And you'd be surprised how many parents have no
idea of the trouble their kids are getting into when
their backs are turned. I'm going to talk to this girl
named Malaka." He led them back to the waiting
room. "Have a seat over there. I'll keep you posted."
He turned and disappeared down the hallway.

Julio's parents sat huddled together on one hard
wooden bench. Romiette's parents sat on another. In
spite of the fact that it was two in the morning,
activity swirled around them, phones rang, officers
scurried back and forth, and no one paid any attention to them. It was like being in a hospital waiting
room. Everyone seemed to have a job to do, everyone was occupied with meaningless activity, and no
one thought to stop to speak to the families sitting
on the hard wooden benches, waiting for any bits of
new information about their children.

Maria Montague's face was swollen and red from
weeping. Her husband was silent, impassive, his face a
mask of pain and loss. She glanced at him, then walked
slowly to where Romiette's parents were sitting.

"Mrs. Cappelle, our children are linked together in

this terrible thing. Let's you and me, the mothers of these children, link ourselves together. Do you pray?"

"Oh, my Lord, yes, Mrs. Montague. I pray. I pray with all my heart."

"Call me Maria."

"And call me Lady. Together we can get through this—and dream our children safely home."

The two fathers looked past each other, never making eye contact. Neither one spoke.

47.

A Lead

Captain Escaluski looked at the girl dressed in purple. Her hair was uncombed, and her purple-painted fingernails were chipped and cracked. She was trying to look hard and tough, but he could see she was scared. He started slowly, casually. "Malaka, do you know what you're being charged with?"

She refused to look at him. "I haven't done anything wrong!" she said to the wall. "You can't prove nothin'! I was just ridin'. You cops is always hasslin' us."

"The car you were in may have been used in a crime—a kidnapping—perhaps even a murder. If that proves to be the case, you will be charged as an accessory to that murder, and you can be charged as an adult. So we're talking—let's see—at least fifteen, twenty years. You ready to do that kind of time?"

That got her attention. She turned and looked at him with derision. "You trippin'! They wouldn't send a girl to jail. I'm only sixteen. I'd get probation, and they'd send me home," she stated boldly.

"You've been watching too many movies. If you

are convicted of a felony as an adult, you *will* go to jail! The older women there—they look forward to a fresh young girl like you. No one could protect you then. Are you sure that you're ready to go that far for your friends?"

"I don't know why you're tryin' to scare me. I didn't do anything, honest. I was just ridin' in the car with my boyfriend and some of his friends. I didn't have control over where they went or what they did. I was in the backseat." She flicked a speck of dirt off the table.

"In the backseat with a gun? Possession of a firearm itself is a felony, Malaka."

"It's not mine. Terrell gave it to me. To show me he trusted me. I was just holdin' it for him because he said they'd arrest him, but since I was a juvenile, they couldn't bother me."

"Well, he was wrong there! What else did he tell you?" the captain urged.

"He told me my mama wouldn't come if anything happened. He was right about that."

"What did she say when you talked to her?"

"She said she was tired, and she had warned me about hanging with Terrell, and to teach me a lesson, she was gonna make me spend the night here! Me and my mama don't get along. That's why I been living with my dad. But he ain't home."

"Here's a Kleenex. Don't cry. Relax now. Terrell and the rest of them are in custody. The only way you're going to get out of the mess you're in is to help us out here. Can you do that?"

"They were gonna let me in the gang. It sounded so cool."

"Which gang?"

"The Devildogs. They the baddest gang in the city right now," Malaka boasted.

"Gangs are pretty new here."

"That's why it's important to get in early and tight. At least that's what Terrell told me. At school, they won't even admit that gangs exist! It's funny. That way, we do what we want and nobody really stops us."

"Do you know anything about the disappearance of Romiette and Julio?"

"No." Malaka turned away.

"Are you sure? Romiette's mother said you talked to her and it sounded like you might know something."

"I really don't know anything. Really."

"Well, you had your chance. You will be charged with possession of a firearm, and if we find them, kidnapping, assault, and who knows what else? Maybe even murder. Is your boyfriend worth all that?"

"I didn't kill nobody!" Malaka screamed. "Can you get my father to come down here? And a lawyer? I'm getting scared."

"I'll call both your parents. And you have the right to a lawyer. I will inform them, or a lawyer will be provided for you. In the meantime, please, just tell us where to start looking. The DA will look kindly on any help you give. Besides, there's a five-thouand-dollar reward out. Did you know that?"

Malaka slumped in her chair. It was the middle of the night, and she was tired. Things had not gone according to plan, and she wasn't going to take Terrell's rap. She sighed and said finally, "I never wanted it to go this far. I just wanted the gang boys to like me. Me and my mother don't get along, and everybody in the gang really liked me, or they seemed to. Terrell was big and tough and so much fun to be with. He kept teasing me about what a wimp I was. I wanted to show him I was tough enough. I showed him too," she said with pride.

"Are you tough enough to tell the truth?" the captain asked.

Malaka thought for moment. "You know the boathouse by London Woods Lake?"

"Yeah."

"Look around there." She rested her head on the table.

Captain Escaluski sighed as he closed the door. He called dispatch and told them to concentrate the search in and around the London Woods boathouse. He knew the parents would be relieved to get even a small lead. He also knew that the longer those kids were missing, the less chance there would be of finding them alive. That part he wasn't ready to share with the parents. He walked into the waiting room, and they jumped up, eyes full of hope.

"Mr. and Mrs. Montague, Mr. and Mrs. Cappelle, we may have a lead. The girl Malaka told us what she knew. It seems that the original plan was just to scare them. Evidently, the gang didn't like the idea of

Romiette and Julio seeing each other. Their plan was to threaten or force the two of them to break up."

"With guns?" Maria Montague said in disbelief.

"Evidently, yes."

"What do they care? Why, Captain?" Romi's mother was searching for a reason to make sense of all this.

The captain shrugged. "Who knows? They don't need a reason. Sometimes just being different is reason enough to hate."

"That's stupid."

"Yes, but unfortunately, all too true." A uniformed officer whispered something in the captain's ear. "I'll be right back," he said. He disappeared behind a door. The parents looked at one another in shared fear. Maria Montague and Lady Cappelle grasped each other's hands.

The officer returned holding a sheet of paper. He cleared his throat. "My men were at the boathouse when I sent the dispatch. They searched it thoroughly. I'm sorry, but your children aren't there." Maria Montague inhaled sharply. "But we think that they were. On the gravel near the boathouse, we found two key chains hooked onto one ring—one that says Texas Rangers, and a gold one with the initials RRC."

"That's Romi's. I gave it to her last year for her birthday!" her mother said with excitement. It was her first ray of hope in this dark night.

"And that's Julio's key chain. He collects Texas Rangers stuff." Maria Montague smiled broadly for the first time that night. "You say the key chains were hooked together?" she asked.

"Yes, on the same key ring, the report says," the captain read. "Folks, my officers also report that there's a boat missing from the boathouse. We have all our force out there looking. We'll find them, I promise, but we have another problem. That's a pretty bad storm out there. The wind is awful—heavy rain, thunder, lightning. We may not be able to do much more searching tonight."

"What do you mean, 'not much more tonight'! You've got to get out there and find my child!" Luis Montague yelled.

"Yes, sir, Mr. Montague. We're doing our best."

Romi's mother looked frantic. "Captain," she said. "There's something you should know."

"Yes, Mrs. Cappelle?"

"Romiette can't swim."

The captain looked up in surprise and scribbled a note on his pad. He told the families, "I want you all to go home and get some sleep now. We have a long day of searching tomorrow, and I know you want to help. I want you fresh and rested." They looked at him doubtfully. He knew they wouldn't sleep—couldn't sleep. "Go home and pray, then. I'll see all of you back here first thing in the morning. And if we have any news—anything at all—I'll call you. You have my word. Now go."

He left the parents standing there, dazed and confused. Luis walked to the door of the police station, looked out at the storm, and returned to his place on the bench. "I can't leave," he said simply. "If there is any word at all, I want to be at this place to hear it." His wife sat beside him. The Cappelles looked at each other and silently agreed as well. Romiette's mother collapsed in tears in her husband's arms. The visions of guns and pain and violence on her daughter's body were too large to hold in any longer and hope was quickly evaporating. Cornell held her gently until the wave of anguish subsided. Luis and Maria watched in silent understanding.

The Cappelles and the Montagues waited for the light of morning. The night had never been darker.

48.

Ben and Destiny—
Midnight

Destiny opened her front door and flopped dejectedly on the living-room couch. Ben, nervous and tense, kept biting his fingernails and running his hands through his hair. He called his mother, told her briefly only that one of his friends was missing and he was going to help find him, then continued to pace and bite his nails. Destiny's mother had already left to see what she could do to help.

Destiny, for once, was silent. Ben glanced at her and grinned in spite of himself. Destiny was not the kind of girl he usually imagined himself with. She was loud, outspoken, and saw the world through other-colored glasses, not like the rest of them. But, then, so did he. He imagined himself sitting on the couch next to her. What a picture they would make! He, with safety pins and blue or green or orange hair, pale white skin, freckles, blue eyes. And Destiny, skin the color of dark Arabian coffee, hair done in braids and curls, brown eyes, spicy smile, soft lips . . . He forced himself to erase the picture. Right now, the problem was finding Romi and Julio. His foolish dreams could wait.

"What can we do, Destiny?" he asked her, mind racing at all the horrible possibilities.

"There's only one thing we can do," Destiny said simply. "We have to go find them."

"You're right. Romi and Julio are out there in this storm somewhere, maybe hurt, but needing us for sure," Ben agreed. "Go get some rain gear and let's get busy."

Destiny ran upstairs, braids bouncing behind her, to find the rain boots that she once told her mother she'd never wear because they were ugly, and a rain-coat. Once again, Ben found himself watching her body as she danced lightly up the stairs. He knew she thought of him as just a friend, and a strange one at that. He sighed and jumped back into his role as freaky sidekick as she came back down the steps. She carried two flashlights, an extra rain jacket for Ben, and a portable CD player.

"Might be a long night. We'll need music." Ben grinned in agreement. She ran into the kitchen, grabbed several apples and pears, and a bottle of water. "OK, where do we start?"

"Don't you think the police have thought of this already, Destiny? Aren't they searching too?"

"Yeah, but we *care*. I can't just sit and wait for news. Romi is my very best friend, and I have to go and try to help her. She needs me."

"I'm with you, Destiny. Let's do it." Ben didn't want to tell Destiny that the news would probably not be good. The Devildogs could be brutal.

"Let's see," Destiny mused. "We were pushing the

car and we could see them about a block and a half ahead of us. We'll start there—at the spot where we saw them last."

"Then what?" Ben wondered. "London Woods is huge."

"My guess would be to head to the lake. That's what my strongest psychic hunch tells me. I don't know why."

"Then that's where we'll go," Ben said. "I trust you. And I don't know why."

Destiny laughed as they headed out the door into the rain. "But this time we take *my* car, bet?"

"Bet." Ben grinned.

They drove through the rain in silence, the windshield wipers whispering, "Help me, help me." Destiny thought of Romi and their friendship and refused to think what Romi might be enduring at this moment, refused to consider the possibility that she might never see her again. Ben mused how grateful he was to find such a good friend in Julio. Because of his independent attitude about most things, Ben had few close friends, and he realized now how much Julio's honest acceptance of him meant.

They approached the place where Romi and Julio had vanished. Destiny stopped her car, and they got out. It was pouring rain, and the ground was muddy and messy.

"Look! Here's what's left of the tire tracks of a big car, I think," Ben noted. "Probably Terrell's Cadillac."

"Hard to tell with all this rain. So you think they took them in the car?"

"Yeah, but I don't think they took them for a scenic ride. This is kidnapping, Destiny," Ben said solemnly as they hurried back to her car.

"I know. We've gotta hurry. I have a bad feeling about this. Let's follow the road around the park, first of all. Then we'll get out and walk where my senses tell me to."

Even though the road was paved, it was narrow, and the rain made the shadows of the trees loom tall and menacing. They drove, not expecting to find Julio and Romi in front of them, but hoping to find something that might give them a clue. Nothing had appeared, however. Just rain and wind. "This is a big forest," Ben noted. "Why'd they put a forest in the middle of the city anyway?"

"They didn't," Destiny replied with authority. "The forest was here first. This is all that's left of the original woods that were here when people started cutting down trees to build houses and schools and fast-food restaurants."

"You're probably right." Ben sighed. "What time is it?"

"After midnight, I know." Destiny glanced at the clock on the dashboard. "Oh, Ben, it's 1:11! Make a wish!"

"What?"

"Make a wish. Don't ask why. Just do it."

"OK, I wish we—"

"No! You can't tell! Wish silently. When a digital clock reads the same three numbers across, you make a wish."

"That's stupid, I think."

"Just shut up and wish. Don't question the universe!"

"OK, I wished. Who am I to question the mysteries of the great beyond?" Ben asked with cheerful exaggeration. "Did you wish?"

"Of course."

"Do I have to clap my hands three times and hold my breath so Tinkerbell won't die?"

"Don't make fun of this, Ben. It works." Destiny tried to act offended, but grinned in spite of herself.

"OK, whatever you say," Ben replied, but she didn't think he was too convinced. "Destiny," Ben said as he tried to get his bearings in the rain and darkness, "pull over right here."

She stopped the car, and they sat silently for a moment, listening to the thunder and rain, and watching the storm as it rumbled through the woods. "Should we get out and search now?" she asked Ben.

"Yeah, but we don't need to be walking so close to all these trees in a thunderstorm. Lightning strikes trees, you know."

"Actually," she teased, "lightning is drawn more to metallic objects, like earrings and safety pins!"

"Ouch!" Ben twitched and writhed as if he had been hit.

The thunder roared and exploded around them, and lightning flashed, brightening the sky just enough to show the dark, heavy clouds for a moment. The rain poured in sheets, and the windshield wipers could not keep up. The car windows began to fog up. Destiny rolled the windows down just a little to let in some air, but the rain forced itself through the tiny cracks.

"I guess we'd better wait a few minutes. We can't do them any good if we can't even see where we're going. We could walk right past them and never know it," Ben said reasonably.

"I wonder where they are, Ben," Destiny moaned. "What if they're out in this? What if they're wet and scared and lost? What if they're hurt?" Destiny started to cry.

"Tomorrow when the sun is shining, we'll look back on all this as a great adventure, and the four of us will laugh. You'll see, Destiny," Ben said, trying to comfort her. He reached over and touched her hand. She didn't pull it away until she had to find a tissue to blow her nose.

"Hey, Ben," Destiny said slowly. "Suppose they're . . . they're . . . not OK."

"You mean dead?"

"Yeah, dead. It's hard to say the word."

"I don't know, Destiny. I talk big, but I've never seen death up close."

"Me either. I get the chills just thinking about it." She shivered.

"You cold, Destiny?"

"A little."

"Here, take my coat."

"Thanks. What about you?"

"I got a sweatshirt on. I'm OK."

Ben glanced at Destiny in the darkness. She sat huddled in his jacket, her face a mask of fear and worry. He knew as she watched the storm that she was visualizing Romi and Julio and trying to imagine what it was like for them, and where they might be on this terrible night. Ben was glad that he was fairly dry, sitting in Destiny's car, and experiencing the fury of a storm with the faint smell of her hair spray in the air.

She asked him, "Ben, you ever think about what they're saying on the news about Romi and Julio having names like Romeo and Juliet?"

"Yeah, that's something. It's heavy the way they fell for each other so quick."

"Were there any gangs in the play?" asked Destiny.

"Not really," Ben told her. "The families hated each other, and everybody in town sided with one family or the other, just like gangs do, but the play ends with death. Lots of death."

"Well, this is real life, Ben," Destiny whispered. "I don't think I could deal with death like they did in the play."

"I hope you don't have to," he said sincerely.

They talked quietly as they listened to the rain. Ben dozed a few minutes, and Destiny did as well. They were afraid to run the motor very long, but the inside of the car was warm enough. Destiny woke up, startled, with a particularly loud blast of thunder.

"Wow! That was a big one! But it seems like it's letting up a bit," she noted as the rain's steady drumming on the hood of the car began to diminish a bit.

"I'm tired," she added, "and a little hungry too."

"It seems like we've been waiting in this car for hours." Ben stretched his arms and legs as far as the cramped confines of the car would allow. He glanced at the clock. "It's 2:20. No wonder we're tired—and hungry."

"Oh, my goodness!" exclaimed Destiny. "Get ready to wish!"

"You got to be kidding! Again?" Ben looked at Destiny as if she had lost her mind.

"I'm serious as a heart attack!" Destiny fixed her eyes on the clock for another minute. "Okay. 2:22. Wish!" she commanded.

"OK! OK! I'm wishing!"

"Me too. Did you wish the same wish as last time?" Destiny sighed with relief that they had not missed it.

"Yep. You want to know what I wished for?"

"No, don't tell me, or it won't come true," Destiny warned.

"Well, I wouldn't want that to happen," Ben said, and smiled, then he changed the subject. "I think the rain has slowed down enough to get out and walk and search some more. I'll feel better knowing at least we tried to look for them. Let's head down to the lake. It's down that walkway."

Destiny agreed, and they gathered their flashlights and rain gear and headed out into the wet, dark night.

49.

Romiette and Julio—
The Ordeal

The old sweatshirt that was pulled over Romi's head hadn't been washed in a while and smelled of sweaty male. She screamed, but the sound was muffled. She was held tightly by two sets of very strong arms as she was carried away from Julio and toward—what, she did not know. She could hear Julio kicking and fighting behind her, but the sounds were distant, and when they forced her into the backseat of a car, the two back doors slammed, and she couldn't hear him anymore. Two silent bodies sat next to her, holding her arms and preventing any movement. When she tried to kick at one of them, he kicked her shin as hard as he could. She refused to cry out, but silent tears fell from her eyes behind the dirty sweatshirt.

She could hear the trunk of the car being opened, muffled sounds of scuffling and cursing, and then a thud as something was tossed into the trunk. She knew it was Julio. She prayed he was safe. The trunk slammed, the car doors opened, the rest of the four gang members squeezed in, and the car sped off. It had all happened in two minutes.

No one spoke. They knew where they were headed. Romi strained to hear sounds of movement from the trunk, but she could hear nothing. The car turned left three times, then drove over what seemed to be a gravel roadway. She could hear the crunching under the tires and the ping of stone against metal as the pebbles hit the car. They slowed to a stop.

The gang members opened the car doors. Romi was pushed from one side and pulled to the other as she was forced from the car. She could just see the gravel under her feet from where the sweatshirt over her head had twisted a bit. She could smell the water nearby. She started to panic. Since they hadn't driven very far, Romi figured they were near London Woods Lake. It was a large lake, popular with fishermen and boaters in the summer. But at this time of year, it was cold, bleak, and virtually deserted.

Romi had never been so scared in her life. She trembled as she stood there, afraid to run because of the guns she knew they had, afraid to call out to Julio, but alert, listening, and ready to take advantage of whatever might happen. No magical chances appeared. She heard them open the trunk and grunt as they lifted Julio out. There was no sound from him, and Romi could detect no movement. The two guards still held her tightly. She couldn't even turn her head to listen for a flicker of noise or action from him. She only heard the dull thud of Julio's body being dropped on the gravel about three feet from her. She started to tremble uncontrollably. Julio couldn't be dead! There was no gunshot, and he hadn't been in the trunk long enough to lose consciousness. But no sound came from the direction of where she knew he lay.

Suddenly her arms were jerked tightly behind her. She cried out in pain as they tied the ropes around her wrists and arms. The hood was pulled tighter over her face, making her breath come in short, shallow gasps as she struggled for air through the fabric. They dragged her then to what she knew was the edge of the water. As she struggled, one of her shoes came off. Her terror grew. Fear for Julio, fear of what they would do to her, and fear of the water made her struggle frantically as they forced her down the path. She screamed, her breath puddling in hot gasps inside the sweatshirt over her face. Still, they pushed her toward the water.

Romiette felt herself being lifted into something hard and wooden. It smelled wet and moldy, and was damp as her knees landed on it. She knew it was a boat when they made her kneel in the bottom of it, head down, arms tied hind her back. She felt them wrap more rope around her as they tied her, still kneeling, to the seat of the boat. She could not move. Her knees hurt, her back began to throb, and her shoulders ached as she lay there tied in the bottom of the damp wooden boat. She was weeping loudly now, begging for mercy, for a loosening of the ropes, for help. Still no one spoke. All was silent.

She heard them lift Julio next with silent grunts. They seemed to be tying him just as they had tied her, on the other side of the center seat. She could hear a muffled groan as Julio began to regain consciousness. Romi cheered and thought that perhaps there was hope after all. She willed him to speak, to gain strength, to throw off these devils who were hurting them. She knew he could do it! Then, she heard a thunk as they hit him in the back of his head once more. He dropped, ceased to struggle, and once again, all was silent. All she could hear was her own sobbing tears and the lapping of the waves against the side of the boat.

They pushed the boat into the water then. Romiette screamed in terror. To be in this much water, with night approaching, tied helplessly in the bottom of a boat, was more than she could bear. She pulled at the ropes, hysterical now, as she felt the boat begin to bounce upon the waves of the lake. She pulled and strained every muscle, using every ounce of her strength to get free, to get away from the terror. She heard one of the gang members splash into the water with a curse. Then a bright, throbbing pain exploded at the base of her neck and Romi was silent and still.

The car sped away, gravel rattling the bottom of it as it headed back to the main road. Silence settled on the scene. The night crept quietly and deeply over the lake. Darkness filled the small wooden boat in which Romiette and Julio floated helplessly. A faint rumble of thunder threatened in the distance.

50.

The Dream and the Reality

It was the dream. Romi knew she'd have to call her mother for this one. Every muscle in her body ached. Her shoulders were screaming, her knees throbbed, and she couldn't breathe. She felt the terror, but didn't feel the water. She smelled it, but there were no flames. This dream was different, and much worse. Romi groaned, and her eyes opened suddenly. All was darkness. She reached for her bedroom light, but her arms wouldn't budge, She could hear thunder in the distance, could feel a stiff breeze on her back. Had she left the window open? She struggled to wake up and then the pain in her head returned, and she remembered. She began to weep as she remembered it all: the ropes, the boat, the fear, the cruel blow to the back of her head, and Julio. Was he alive?

She struggled to speak. "Julio! Julio!"

All was silent. Julio did not move. Although she could do nothing with the ropes that held her, Romi found that if she twisted her head from side to side, the sweatshirt over her face moved a bit. Slowly she shook it off, like a dog shakes off a hated collar. The cool night air rushed into her lungs, and she breathed deeply and thankfully. It was pitch dark. No moon shone in the cloud-covered sky, and the rumblings of thunder were becoming loud and powerful. She couldn't tell how far into the lake they had floated; she couldn't see either shore. The air was as black as the sky and water. It was cold, and a few hard, dark raindrops hit her back. No hope floated with them. Romi wept.

The rain began to pelt them, and the wind increased. The boat rocked helplessly in the water, and Romi screamed in terror once again. Julio stirred and groaned, the cold water and wind forcing him into consciousness. He gasped for breath as Romi had, and Romi let hope enter her heart once more.

"Romi! Please be OK," Julio pleaded.

"Yes, Julio, I am. My arms hurt where the ropes are too tight, my knees and shoulders are killing me, but I think I'm OK. I'm so scared, Julio. What about you? Are you OK?"

"I think so," Julio replied groggily. "We gotta get loose, get these ropes off. Big storm coming, Romi." Dazed and silent for a moment, he tried to make his mind think clearly.

"What are we going to do, Julio?" Romi's voice jarred him back to reality. "I'm sure our parents are looking for us, and the police are too. They are, don't you think?" Romi asked, suddenly doubtful.

"Sure, they're looking," Julio said, trying to reassure her, "but do you think they'll find us? If we're on London Woods Lake, it's big, and it's dark, and it's getting ready to storm."

"They'll never find us in a storm," Romi said, worried. "I wonder what time it is. My head hurts."

"They'll find us—don't worry. Or if not, we'll find a way out of here ourselves," Julio said with a certainty he didn't feel.

"Out of a boat in the middle of the lake? I can't swim, Julio! I can't swim! I'm so afraid. All that blue and nothing to hold on to."

The small boat rocked on the increasingly strong waves of the lake. They could hear the sloshing of the water on the sides. Water splashed into the boat, and the rain pelted them from above. Julio said quietly, "Hey, Romi! Remember our talk about adventures and fantasies? Well, we've got a real one on our hands here. I'm a good swimmer, remember, and remember this—I won't let anything happen to you, you got that?"

Romi didn't know whether to cry or to giggle. "If I wasn't so scared and stiff and didn't hurt so bad," she said to Julio in the darkness, "I think I'd like the idea of being curled up in the bottom of a boat with you!"

"You're a sick puppy, Romiette."

"Why did they do this to us, Julio? I'm so scared."

"Who knows? Right now we've got to get loose. Let's see if we can wriggle out of these ropes. Can you move your hand at all?"

She tried, but her hands, wet and cold, wouldn't cooperate. "I can't move my fingers!" she wailed.

"My hands are numb. My whole body is soaked and freezing. I'm so cold. I can't do anything! We're going to die here."

"We are *not* going to die here. Now force yourself. Wiggle those fingers and pull at the end of your rope. There you go. That's better."

Romi worked silently as she struggled with her bonds. She could hear Julio's breathing, raspy and thin, as he labored to do the same. Then she said quietly, "I'm scared, Julio."

"I am too, Romi. But we are going to get out of this. I swear to you. The ropes on my hands are almost untangled. I think this is the last one." Julio sat up slowly and painfully, rubbing his arms and wrists, thankful for the rain that fell and cooled the rope burns.

Romi managed to loosen the last of her rope as well. Julio helped undo the ropes tying her to the boat. "I'm free," she told him victoriously. As she tried to sit up, she groaned, "Oh, the pain. Julio, I can hardly move."

"Me either. But I think we're gonna have to move quickly. This storm is getting pretty bad."

Lightning, which had flashed in the distant sky, was now right above them. Trees in the distance stood like gaunt sentinels of the lake, brightly illuminated by the fierce flashes. Another streak of fire pierced the sky and pointed itself at one of the trees. It glowed, then flashed, then cracked and burned like firewood. For a moment it was a torch, then the rain and wind doused the flame and the smell of burning wood drifted across to Romiette and Julio, who huddled together in the bottom of the little boat. As the wind intensified and churned the water, the small boat was tossed about mercilessly. Rolling explosions of thunder shook the sky, the earth, and the water. The whole world shook with noise and power. Finally the rain pelted them with fury. Lightning sizzled as it struck the water, and the lake itself seemed to be contorted in anger. Julio and Romiette sat huddled together, terrified, trembling, tossing in the bottom of the boat.

"Can you die of noise, Julio?" Romi asked between bursts of thunder and flashes of lightning.

"I don't know if noise ever killed anybody, but fear sure did." Once more the thunder exploded above their heads.

"I've never seen lightning up close like this before," Romi exclaimed, amazed at the spectacle in spite of her fear. "It's so wild. Like God spitting fire from his fingernails!"

"And then crashing mountains together!" Julio said in awe. Both of them realized the danger they were in. "We've got to get out of this boat, Romi," Julio said with certainty.

Romi's heart quickened. Fear spoke first. "I'm not getting out of this boat! You must be crazy! If I get out of the boat and in the water, I will die! No doubt about it—I'm just gonna sink to the bottom and die!"

"Not if I can help it. Let's see now, where are the oars—they ought to be attached to the side, right?" Julio felt for the place where the oars ought to be.

"I can't see much, but I don't think there are any oars here, Julio."

"They took them, of course." Julio sighed.

"Now what?" Romi asked.

"Are your hands still stiff from the ropes, Romi?"

"They're OK. What do you want me to do?"

"Let's see if we can paddle this thing by hand." They each moved to a side of the small boat and placed their hands in the cold water. On a summer day, streaming a hand in the water playfully was a pleasant and soothing experience. But their hands soon became numb as they tried to move the boat in the frigid, churning water. The boat made no progress.

"It's raining so hard and the lightning is so close!" Romi yelled through the downpour.

Julio had been in storms in a boat before, but never a storm this intense, and never alone. He knew they were a sure target for a bolt of lightning. "We gotta get out of this boat, and off this water, Romi! That lightning is too sharp and too close. It's gonna hit us!"

"I can hardly hear you! The thunder is roaring so much! The whole world is exploding!" screamed Romi. She laughed then, in spite of the situation. Julio, curly hair dripping, drenched and weary, was illuminated for a moment by the lightning. He looked awful. She knew she didn't look much better. "Look at us, Julio! And to think I worried this afternoon about how my hair would look for you."

Julio looked at Romi's matted hair and soaked clothes and tossed more water on her. They both laughed so hard, they forgot their plight for one brief moment. Then a bolt of lightning speared past them and landed with a flaming, steaming sizzle in a tree about ten feet up the shore. It jarred them back to reality.

"Oh, my Lord! That one was close!" Romi cried, suddenly serious and frightened again.

Julio told her clearly, "We've got to get out of this boat, Romi."

"NO!" she screamed. "I'll drown!"

"I won't let you drown." Julio lowered himself into the freezing water. He gasped at the coldness of it. He held out his hand to her. "Take my hand. Hold on to me. I will not let you go."

"No, Julio, I'm terrified of water. I'll pull you down. I can't do it." She let go of his hand and sat shaking in the boat.

"Romi, the lightning is hitting trees on shore. It will hit this boat. I know it." In the flashes of lightning she could make out his face, pleading and full of concern not for himself but for her. "Come on, Romi. You'll be fine."

Trembling, she seized his hand and let him lead her over the side of the boat. He lowered her slowly and carefully into the water. Romi was stiff with fear and cold. She barely dared to breathe. He helped her grab the side of the boat and bent her numb fingers so she could grasp it better. The water sloshed onto her face and she gasped, but Julio lifted her so her head was above the waterline. "Please don't let me go," she said, trembling.

"I've got you. Relax. I won't let anything happen to you, do you hear me? I love you, Romiette."

"What did you say? The thunder, the noise, the water!"

"*Te amo*. I love you! You're not going to die."

With a crack that split the heavens, a huge bolt of fire was spit from the sky. It arced, twisted, and with vicious rage, the lightning stabbed the small wooden boat. The air smelled of charred wood and the harsh chemical odor of fire between water and sky. Flames, which were quickly extinguished by the driving rain, rose from the gaping hole and tried to spread along the bottom of the boat. Both Romiette and Julio could feel the electricity of the lightning bolt as the small boat was incinerated and crumpled. Her hand was wrenched from his, and he was alone struggling to find the surface. Julio reached for Romi in the darkness, but all was fire and acrid smoke and swirling water. He searched the area, fruitlessly grabbing broken pieces of wood from the boat, hoping that Romi was somehow clinging to one of them. He shouted her name, went under again and again, but Romi was deep within the thing she feared the most—the dark, cold water.

51.

The Reality Is the Dream

Romi tried to think, to scream, to remember. The water seared her thoughts. Thinking became a dream, and remembering a painful reality. Was this reality or a dream?

The thunder roared, the lightning flashed, then thunder exploded once again. She smelled the water then. Deep, evil, powerful. The water had been their only hope, their only chance, their leap into faith, into death. She had screamed. Then all was silence as the water thundered into her ears, forced itself down her throat, and burned its way into her nose, her lungs, her brain. This water was fierce and deadly—no cool, gentle waves, but hot, choking, liquid flames, sucking the breath of life from her. She struggled, searching for air, for land, for something to hold on to. But there was only the water, pulling her into its depths. She couldn't breathe. She couldn't swim. She could no longer scream. The fire cooled, the terror ebbed, and the dark shadow of death embraced her.

She drifted then—in a haze of colors and swirls and black, frightening void. Voices? Could she hear voices? One voice? Maybe it was a song. No, all was silence. Thick, enveloping quiet that led to despair. No reason to care, to breathe, to live. So easy to let the silence swallow her. But the voice pierced the darkness. It was calling her name, grabbing her thoughts, and making her remember the fear, the pain, the cold, clammy water. The water! She gasped, and the water grabbed her once more, viciously dragging her to its depths. But that voice. It floated down to where she lay, cradled in the arms of the victorious water. The voice called her one last time. It was Julio.

52.

Romiette and Julio—
Fire and Water

Julio swam to the surface once more and breathed deeply. It was still raining in strong sheets of water, but the fury of the storm seemed to have subsided. He looked around frantically for Romiette, but he could see so sign of her. He knew she was terrified. This was her nightmare, her fear dream, and he was unable to help her. He plunged beneath the water but, except for the diminishing sound of the thunder as it retreated into the distance, he could hear nothing. He shouted her name, half praying, half pleading to the hidden stars to help him find her.

"Romiette! Romiette!" He dove under the water again, reaching for her, feeling for her, sensing her closeness. He knew he only had a short time to find her. He let himself drift to the bottom of the lake where the darkness of the water was total and complete. The only thing that led him was his heart, his knowledge that he would never leave that lake without her. His lungs were burning fire, about to explode, when he touched her arm. She was floating facedown, her hair caught on a jagged rock. He touched her face, gently freed her, and swam with her to the surface.

He gasped frantically, and let her face feel the night air. The rain had stopped, the lightning was merely a distant blink, and the air was clear and cold. But Romiette floated in his arms, not breathing, unaware of the life it offered. Julio shouted her name again. "Romiette!" Silence, except for the echo of his voice on the water. He could see the shore now, and swam as swiftly as he could, calling her name, the only raindrops now his tears of fear and anguish. He knew that they could both die of hypothermia if they didn't get out of that water right away. It seemed like hours, but only a few minutes had passed since they had lost each other in the storm. He reached the shore, half lifted, half dragged her from the water, and laid her gently on the ground. He forgot about the pain in his arms and back and head. He forgot about how cold he was. His only thought was to make her breathe, to make her live. He tried to remember all the steps of CPR as he breathed into her mouth and compressed her chest. He couldn't tell if she was dead or just unconscious. She lay in the mud, unmoving, and Julio shouted curses to the stars. ·

The wind blew hard, much colder now that the rain had stopped, and Julio knew he could do no more. He shivered uncontrollably in the darkness and looked for shelter. He was dizzy, weak, and was starting to fade into unconsciousness himself. He picked up Romiette's cool, damp body and stumbled as far as he could into the woods. He tripped over a huge tree that had fallen many storms before, and almost dropped Romi as he landed in a hollow under it. He gently placed Romi on the spongy pine needles and leaves, then squeezed himself into the shallow hole next to her. He pulled Romiette as close to himself as he could. At least there was a bit of shelter from the wind, he thought vaguely. He tried to concentrate, but he was so tired, and the air was so cold. It was easy to rest for a bit. Julio shivered, hugged Romi closer to him, and faded into sleep.

53.

Police Investigation—
5 A.M.

Captain Escaluski frowned and scratched what was left of his thinning hair. He didn't like this one. His men had been out all night, tromping through rain and mud, but able to do very little. All of the gang members except for the girl refused to make any statements at all—their code of silence, he assumed. His thoughts were interrupted by a call from Will Spear, his chief field investigator.

"Captain, this is Will. We found something, and it's not good."

Escaluski braced himself. "What is it?" he asked quickly.

"We found pieces of a boat, broken and floating, out here on the far end of the lake. It was charred and burned—a big hole burned right through the center of it. Looks like it had been struck by lightning."

"Any sign of the kids?"

"No, Captain, just dark, stormy water." Officer Spear paused. "Sir, I think you better order the lake-dragging equipment."

Escaluski sighed. "Already done, Will. You don't think they tried suicide like in the Shakespeare story, do you?" He was trying to cover all possibilities. "Maybe they were scared of the gang and tired of all the opposition to their relationship, and they decided to off themselves. It's happened before. Any sign they were in that boat, Will?"

"Nothing yet, but if they *were* in that boat, we might have a case of murder instead. I sure hope not. They seemed to be nice kids."

"Nice, yes; but stupid, maybe."

"Either way," Officer Spear summarized, "we've got a big thunderstorm, an unsearchable lake, two missing kids, and no bodies."

"Yet," added Escaluski, who had seen far too many unhappy endings to stories such as this one. He sighed again. "Thanks, Spear. Stay on it. Report to me anything you find."

"Yes, sir."

At that moment another officer knocked on the captain's door. He was young, had only been on the force a few weeks, and was just one-quarter of an inch taller than the minimum requirement to be a police officer. Escaluski chuckled as he watched the new guy walk—it seemed as if he tiptoed everywhere—trying to make himself look taller. "Excuse me, sir, Officer Balzar here. I found something, sir, that I think might be important in this investigation." He was almost trembling with excitement.

"What have you got, Balzar?" the captain questioned, smiling at his youthful enthusiasm.

"I went back and searched the trunk of the car once more, sir," he explained. "The one that the alleged gang members were arrested in?"

"Yes, I know the car," the captain said impatiently. "What did you find?"

"I crawled into the trunk, uh, since I'm gifted with small stature, sir, and I found this in the back." He handed the captain a tiny video recorder, the one that had fallen from Julio's pocket when they tossed him in the trunk.

Captain Escaluski looked at the camera and heartily thanked the young officer. "I think you've found the key piece of evidence, Balzar! Great detective work!"

Balzar beamed. The captain hurried to the lab to see if his men could run the tape. Perhaps this would help them find the missing teenagers.

54.

Ben and Destiny—5 A.M.

Destiny and Ben tromped through the mud and diminishing rain, searching, but having no idea where to look. They looked under branches, in shallow caves, in all the picnic areas, even the trash Dumpsters. They could tell when the police had been through an area—it was well worn and flattened by several pairs of boots—but they never came into direct contact with the small police search team that worked through the storm and the night. Ben made Destiny rest back at the car a couple of times, but they spent most of the night searching for hope, and finding very little.

Destiny had called her mother on the car phone a couple of times, so they knew the police had found the key chain at the boathouse, and that the Devildogs had been arrested. A dull gray dawn was beginning to appear.

Destiny stretched and said to Ben, "Let's check near the boathouse one more time, now that we can see a little better."

"What do you think we can find that the police can't?" Ben grumbled.

"You've been watching too many TV shows, Ben." Destiny grinned. "Maybe they missed something." She beamed the flashlight toward the bushes on the walkway that led from the boathouse to the water.

"See anything?" Ben asked, without much faith.

Destiny screamed, "Ben, com'ere! Where's the other flashlight?"

Ben ran to her. "Hey! What's this?" Ben held up a brown shoe, caked with mud, that was lodged behind a bush.

"It's Romi's shoe!" screamed Destiny. "No, it's my shoe—I loaned it to her. Gee, that seems like so long ago. Oh, Ben, they were here! Do you think they're in the water? Maybe they drowned. Romi can't swim, Ben!"

"We'll find them," he soothed her. "Now, don't start crying. I can't deal with it."

"Wait! The shoe feels cold and damp! I'm getting psychic vibes!"

"The shoe is talking to you?"

"Yeah. You know I'm psychic, don't you?"

"That's what you keep telling people. What does the shoe say? You know it could be just the fact that the shoe was in the mud that it feels cold and damp to you."

"No, it's more than that. Let's go down to the water. I sense fire and water." Destiny walked down to the edge of the water, the place from where boats were launched.

"When that storm hit, there were lots of lightning strikes, so you might be right. Let's start walking around the lake and see if we can spot anything," Ben suggested. "Shine the flashlight on the water. Do you see anything, Destiny?"

"No, let's keep walking." She sighed. "Wait, what's that?" She pointed to a dark shadow on the surface of the lake.

"Just a tree branch in the water—probably broke off in the storm," Ben said.

"I'm hungry," exclaimed Destiny after a few minutes of walking. "That fruit was gone too long ago."

"I thought you were starting a new diet," Ben teased her.

"You remember I said that?"

"I remember everything you say, Destiny."

"Why?"

"No reason. You tired?"

"No, but we're not going back until we find them," she said firmly.

"Goes without saying," agreed Ben. "Let's keep walking. Let's use both flashlights. We've got to spot something."

"I feel so helpless, Ben," moaned Destiny.

"What happened to your psychic vibes?" he asked, trying to cheer her up.

"They fizzled. We're probably too late anyway."

"Quit talking like that, Destiny. What time is it?"

"Ten minutes to six in the morning. I'm tired, and hungry, and scared. We've been here all night long!"

"So have they," Ben reminded her quietly.

"I'm so afraid the morning will bring bad news."

"That was some storm last night, wasn't it?"

"Yeah, I'm glad I had you to share it with. I wasn't even scared." Destiny smiled at Ben with honest appreciation.

"Talk about percussion! Wow! How mighty is the power of nature!" Ben raised both his arms to the sky in exultation.

"Now, don't you go telling people we spent the night together!" warned Destiny, laughing.

"Well, we did."

"Yeah, but . . ."

"Destiny! Check it out. We've caught all five! What do you call it—the Fantastic Five?"

"Oh, my goodness! I almost forgot! We got 1:11 and 2:22."

"Then we remembered 3:33 and 4:44."

"And now it's almost 5:55!"

"Wish, Destiny, wish!"

"You mean you believe that stuff now, Ben?"

"I don't know what I believe. All I know is that you made me wish four times in a row and I'm not going to miss this last one—especially if it means that our wishes will come true. Now, shut up and wish!"

"Wishing!" Destiny exclaimed with a big smile.

"We did it, Destiny! We wished on five in a row. So what does that mean?"

"They say that—"

"Who are 'they'?"

"Smart people, probably women, Romi says," explained Destiny. "Anyway, they say that if you catch five in a row, your wish is guaranteed to come true, and you get an extra wish granted as a special bonus prize."

"Can you tell your wish now?"

"I think so," Destiny frowned, trying to remember the rules. "What did you wish, Ben?"

"I wished that Romiette and Julio be found safely, of course. What about you?"

"I wished the same thing. Do you think this will work?" she asked hopefully.

"What happened to your faith in the universe?" he teased.

"It got cold and hungry and scared in the darkness of the night."

"I still believe in you, Destiny," Ben said, looking directly in her eyes. "And in the universe and magic wishes too." He looked away quickly, and threw a rock in the lake.

"You're something else, Ben," Destiny remarked, pretending not to notice his look. "What was your extra wish for?"

"You."

"Me?"

"I think you're dynamite, Destiny."

"Do I have to dye my hair blue if I hang out with you?"

"Only if it matches your outfit."

"Hey, I like your style!" They grinned at each other as the sky became brighter with the morning sun.

In the distance, near the boathouse, they could see movement as the police and other search teams began for the day. "Let's go see if anyone else has had any better luck in finding anything," Destiny suggested.

"Maybe they have some coffee back at the boathouse," Ben added. "Are you still cold, Destiny?"

"Much warmer now," she said quietly. They marched back along the shore of the lake. Destiny carried Romi's shoe in one hand. Ben held her other hand.

55.

The Parents—6 A.M.

Lady Cappelle stretched and yawned, then woke up suddenly. The horror of last night engulfed her as soon as she opened her eyes. The parents had spent most of the night at the station calling friends and organizations who could assist in a full-scale search as soon as the day would allow. They had made and copied posters, which were ready to be distributed to stores and nailed on telephone poles in the community. Keeping busy had helped keep the fear at bay for a while. Romi's mother had only dozed a minute, but she felt guilty for sleeping even one second while Romi was lost. She glanced at Mrs. Montague, who slept fitfully on the other bench.

"Maria, it's almost dawn," she called. "Wake up."

"Did they find the children, Lady?" Maria replied, startled.

"No, no new word yet," sighed Romi's mother. "I just wanted to be ready for . . . for whatever may come today."

Maria nodded. "I can't believe I fell asleep on those

hard chairs. I didn't think I could sleep at all. Where is my husband?"

"He and Cornell went to get some coffee. They are finally speaking cordially to each other."

"A night in a police station worrying about the lives of one's children erases many foolish notions. Luis loves Julio. He is our only child."

"You know I understand. Romiette is our only daughter." Lady picked up last night's coffee cup and sipped the cold, tasteless liquid.

The two fathers returned with fresh coffee. Captain Escaluski walked with them. He was not smiling.

"Mr. and Mrs. Montague, Mr. and Mrs. Cappelle, as you know, our search last night was frustrating. As much as we could in the storm and darkness, we combed the woods around the lake and found nothing. Our investigation has also turned up another important piece of information, however," he added. "We have located the video camera that the young people mentioned."

Luis gasped. "You have found the camera that was in my son's pocket, but not my son? How can this be?"

The captain explained, "It was found in the trunk of the car that was used in the kidnapping."

"You are sure of that now?" asked Cornell.

"Yes, we have viewed the tape several times." The captain spoke carefully. He didn't want to upset these parents even more. "It seems that the gang members threatened and intimidated your children, then forcibly placed them in their car and took them to what we assume is London Woods Lake. The video portion is fuzzy and dark, but we have very good audio. We have clear identification of each of the Devildogs involved. We can hear sounds of water and the voices of the gang members as they take Julio out of the trunk. There is no more after that," he said quietly.

"The trunk?" Maria gasped. "My Julio was in the trunk? Is he . . . is he alive?" she cried.

"We think he was when they took him out, ma'am. And we have no reason to believe that he isn't still," the captain reassured her. She collapsed in tears.

"And Romi?" her mother asked quietly. "Anything of her?"

"Only at the beginning of the tape, Mrs. Cappelle. We hear her screaming and struggling, and we think she was put in the backseat. That's all the tape tells us."

Lady Cappelle joined Maria on the bench. They shared tissues and hugs.

The captain took a deep breath and continued. "Now that the weather has cleared, and we have daylight, we have two options."

"What's that?" asked Cornell.

"Get volunteers to comb those woods, and to drag the lake."

"Drag the lake?" exclaimed Romi's mother. "Oh, no! That means you think they're dead!"

"No, not at all, Mrs. Cappelle, but it is one way of eliminating that possibility."

"¡Oh, mi Julio! ¡Oh, mi hijo! ¡No. No. No!"

"Maria, it will be all right," her husband soothed her. "We'll find them. At least now we have something to do besides wait."

Cornell was ready for action. "Luis, we've got our equipment ready. Let's head for the lake now. I've got to get out there and find our children."

"Sí, Cornell. We've got blankets, rope, flashlights, a map of the woods. What happened to those pictures of the kids, Maria?"

His wife took the pictures from her pocket. "This is such a wonderful photo of Julio in his band uniform back home." She sighed. "And Romi is such a lovely young woman." She began to weep softly.

"Don't cry, Maria. We are going to find them," Luis reassured her. Luis took the pictures and placed them inside his jacket.

Mrs. Cappelle reminded the men, "I'm going to call the station and make sure the reports go out with every station break, and make sure the news crews are on their way. You two got your cell phone to keep in touch with us?"

"Yes," Cornell replied. "We're out of here. See you up there, Lady B. Our prayers will be answered soon. You'll see."

She wiped her eyes and kissed him quickly. She knew she had to get to work or she'd dissolve in tears. "Maria and I will be out there shortly. We'll be organizing the volunteers from the boathouse. If you find anything at all, buzz my pager."

56.

Morning News Flash—
7 A.M.

Special Bulletin

—Mystery continues to surround the unexplained disappearance of Romiette Cappelle, daughter of TV news anchor Cornell Cappelle, and Julio Montague, transfer student from Corpus Christi, Texas. Are Romiette and Julio lovers like the famous couple of old? Have they run away together? Were they desperate enough to consider suicide, as Shakespeare's characters did? Or are their lives in danger as they hide from the threat of gang violence? Details in a moment.

—The daughter of TV Six newscaster Cornell Cappelle, Romiette Cappelle, age sixteen, and her friend from school Julio Montague, also sixteen, are still missing. They are believed to be lost, perhaps injured, in London Woods Forest. Searches by park police and city police, which were hampered by last night's stormy weather, have been unsuccessful. The two young people were last seen yesterday at dusk, walking near London Woods.

—Five teenagers, all reportedly members of a local gang known sometimes as the Devildogs and sometimes simply as The Family, have been arrested, charged with possession of firearms, and are being questioned in the disappearance of the teens.

—Anyone who has seen Romiette and Julio, or knows anything about their whereabouts, is asked to contact News Six or the district police department. Police are asking for volunteers to help in a detailed, systematic search of the woods. If you are available and would like to help, please call the station at 555–3458, or call the park police at 555-9898. Volunteers should report to the boathouse for maps and instructions. We thank you for your help. Stay tuned to News Six for further details.

57.

Television Interviews

"This is Nannette Norris reporting live from London Woods, on the case of the two missing children. We're going to ask some of the people out here in the field exactly what is going on in the search efforts." Nannette, wearing a pink designer suit and matching shoes, tiptoed daintily in the muddy grass. She carried her portable microphone, and motioned to Lawrence, the cameraman behind her, to hurry. He sighed, shifted the weight of the camera on his shoulder, and followed her to another volunteer.

"Excuse me, sir, this is Nannette Norris, and you're live on TV News Six. How long have you been out here, sir?" She held the mike very close to his mouth. When his voice boomed out, Lawrence had to adjust the sound level.

"I been here since they called for help 'bout two hours ago. Ain't no sign of dem kids—they just gone!"

"Any indication of foul play?" Nannette asked as she switched the mike back to herself quickly.

The volunteer looked at her, squinted his eyes,

and responded, "This ain't no baseball game, lady! This here is life and death! Quit asking stupid, useless questions and help us look. You gettin' in my way!" Nannette signaled to Lawrence with a roll of her eyes that this interview was concluded. Lawrence grinned at the volunteer and gave him a thumbs-up. Nannette moved to her next attempt—a woman, busy answering one of the phones that had been hastily installed that morning by phone company volunteers.

"Excuse me, ma'am, this is Nannette Norris, and you're live on TV News Six. Tell me, ma'am, what's the latest in the search efforts?"

With a phone on one ear, the woman responded, "Well, they're dragging the lake. It's really hard on the parents. They're out there looking with us. The two fathers, Mr. Cappelle and Mr. Montague, are working side by side, checking every tree and every bush to find their kids. I understand there was quite a bit of friction between the two at first."

Nannette's eyes brightened. "Friction? What kind of friction?" She was hoping for a news scoop, an angle that no one else had covered yet.

The woman shrugged. "You know—each one accusing the other of being responsible for this situation. But that's behind them now."

Nannette looked disappointed. "And the mothers of the two young people? How are they taking this?"

The woman was getting annoyed. "They're doing what any mothers would do. They're searching with the rest of us, and praying, and believing—believing that their kids will be returned safely—but the longer we look, the scarier it gets."

"Have you noticed any arguments between the mothers? Any racial insults or name-calling?" Nannette was insistent.

"Are you nuts? What kind of question is that?"

"I just wanted to generate some interest in our viewing public," replied Nannette with insulted pride.

"There's plenty of interest already. People from all races and neighborhoods are working together to find these kids. Why don't you talk about that? Hey, the phones are ringing. I got work to do here."

Nannette smirked as she returned to the microphone. "Well, I can see you're busy. I'll let you get back to your work." The woman ignored her. Lawrence grinned again.

Nannette walked down to the edge of the lake, making sure she stayed on the cemented walkway, not the muddy edges where most of the people worked. She approached a man carrying a plastic garbage bag full of twigs and branches. "Excuse me, sir, this is Nannette Norris, and you're live on TV News Six. Can you tell us how the lake-dragging efforts are going?"

"It's a slow process," he answered. "We've found lots of unbelievable trash, but fortunately, no bodies. But it's a big lake. This will take all day."

"What if you don't find anything?" Nannette insisted.

"Well, that's good, and bad."

"How so?"

"It's good, because we can be fairly sure they didn't drown. But it's bad, because we are running out of other options."

"Are you sure they're here?"

"All indications are that they were here as late as last night before the storm. That's all we know." The man, tired of her insistent questions, tried to walk away.

She continued, "If you find them dead, it'll be pretty gruesome, right?"

He looked as if he wanted to yell at her, but he remembered the camera and simply said, "Excuse me, I've got to get back to work." He marched up to the boathouse for more garbage bags. Nannette followed him. The room was full of bustle and action. Phones rang, people checked maps, and new volunteers arrived every few minutes, asking for assignments and leaving to search a new area. Nannette approached the table where a woman was setting out doughnuts that had been donated by a bakery.

"Excuse me, ma'am, this is Nannette Norris, and you're live on TV News Six. May I ask you a few questions?"

"Sure, if you don't get in my way. I've gotta make some more coffee here for the volunteers."

"Goody. Make mine with two creams and two sugars."

"Aren't you on the air?" the woman asked wryly. Lawrence rolled his eyes.

"Oh, right," Nannette reminded herself. "Tell me, what do you think about the names of the two missing kids? Is the closeness of their names to Romeo and Juliet, and this recent disappearance, just a little similar to the old Shakespearean story?"

"Yeah, it's ironic, but that don't mean nothing." The woman poured the ground coffee into the machine and added fresh water.

"Do you think that Romiette and Julio tried to commit suicide like the lovers in the tale?"

"Why should they do that?" the volunteer asked in surprise. "From what we can tell, they were in love with each other! We're way past the days of arranged marriages, sister. They're in trouble, they need our help, and if you would get out of the way, we might be able to do that." Nannette hurried away as she saw some policemen enter the room. The woman gave Lawrence three doughnuts in a small plastic bag. "Combat pay," she whispered to him, pointing to Nannette. He laughed, thanked her, and agreed with her completely. Nannette motioned to Lawrence to hurry as she spoke to the police officers.

"Excuse me, sir, this is Nannette Norris, and you're live on TV News Six. Officer, can you tell us anything about the reported gang connection to this case?"

"I can't say much. What we know is that there had been some trouble at school between Romiette and Julio and some other students who had been identified as having ties with a local gang. Nothing has been verified, however, and anything else would only be speculation."

"Do you think the lives of Romiette and Julio were threatened or in danger? Some people say they were both involved in gangs." Nannette motioned for Lawrence to do a close-up on her face.

"Aren't reporters supposed to go on more than 'some people say'? As I said, ma'am, anything else would be speculation. Excuse me." The officer walked away. Nannette told Lawrence to cut the close-up, cut the shot completely. Lawrence the Silent smiled once more.

A flurry of activity erupted when Ben and Destiny showed up. Nannette rushed over to the crowd and pushed her way through. "It's Romiette and Julio!" she screamed into the camera. "They've been found!"

Lawrence turned off the camera and said, "Nannette, they've been showing pictures of those kids all day. That's not them!"

"Oh," she said, sniffing. "I knew that. Let's go interview them anyway. I'm sure they know something." She squeezed through the crowd and spoke to Destiny first. "What is your relationship with the two missing teenagers, dear?"

Destiny replied, "I'm Romi's best friend, and please don't call me 'dear.'"

Nannette rolled her eyes and asked, "Are you here to join the search?"

"No, me and Ben have been searching all night. We found Romi's shoe!"

"How do you know it's her shoe? It's pretty muddy," Nannette said doubtfully.

"'Cause it's my shoe—I loaned it to her last week," Destiny told her impatiently.

"And you, son, what's your name and what do you think of this tragedy?"

"My name is Ben, and right now it's not a tragedy." Ben turned away from the camera.

"Did you ever read *Romeo and Juliet* at school?" insisted Nannette.

"Yes, I have," Ben replied, smiling innocently. "Several times. Have you?"

Nannette looked for others to interview, but everyone seemed to be busy working to find Romi and Julio. Nannette then tried to get interviews with Romi's and Julio's parents, but all of them refused. Tired, and angry at the mud on her pink designer shoes, Nannette decided she had had enough for now.

"This is Nannette Norris, reporting live for News Six from London Woods, where the search continues for Romiette Cappelle and Julio Montague. Live updates as the news unfolds."

58.

The Fathers—Noon

Luis and Cornell trudged slowly through the thick weeds and underbrush near the water's edge. They knew that if their children had been in that lake and had somehow been able to get out, they would be somewhere on that muddy shore. The day was bright and cool, but the sun warmed them, and they had removed their jackets. They worked slowly, methodically, checking every rock and tree, grimly determined to find their children.

"Luis, you OK?" Cornell asked as Luis wiped his brow. "Hand me the flashlight. We haven't checked this area."

"*Sí*, Cornell. I'm fine. My lungs are strong, but my heart is becoming heavy. It's almost noon. We should have found them by now."

"Where are Maria and Lady?" Cornell asked, although he knew the answer as well as Luis did. Even idle conversation made thoughts of what they might find more bearable.

"They were searching on the other side of the lake. Together. Just as we are," Luis responded.

"You're right." Cornell hesitated. "Luis, I . . . uh . . . I'm sorry about accusing Julio of whatever it was I said. I wasn't thinking straight. I just am so afraid. I've never been this helpless, and without hope."

"There is always hope, Cornell. The children will be found—alive and well. That is my hope. And my prayer."

"You're very wise, Luis. Let's sit here on this log a minute. You got any more of that water?"

"*Sí,* help yourself. So, what is it like to work with a woman such as Miss Norris? When I went back to the central volunteer area, I heard her asking the most outrageous questions of the volunteers. How is she allowed to get away with such?"

"She is the niece of the executive producer of the show, and even he is running short of patience with her. She's really hard to work with and she just does-n't think before she speaks—and in a reporter, that's a dangerous quality. So it's rough sometimes, really rough. One day we were out together doing a story and she walked up to the mother of a murdered child and asked her where she'd bought her dress! The woman was ready to strangle her."

Luis chuckled. "I think I might have helped her to do it."

"So, do you like Ohio?" Cornell asked him. "Have you made friends?"

"It has been difficult. I have my job, and I have acquaintances, but no real friends. I really miss Texas."

Cornell offered his hand to Luis. Both hands were

covered with mud and dirt from their long morning search. Cornell said clearly, "I would be proud if you'd consider me your friend, Luis."

"Thank you, Cornell. That means so much to me. I hope that our children will also continue to be friends . . . unless—"

"I can't bear to think of anything else," Cornell interrupted. "I'll never give up hope, but it doesn't look good. Two young people reaching out to each other against all odds, against pressure from their peers," he added sadly. "Luis, did you oppose Julio seeing Romiette?"

"At first, I didn't think it was a good idea. It is always easier to stay with what is safe and known."

"I know. I also felt threatened by your son and my daughter. When we first found out about all this last night, my assumption was that he was some kind of Internet freak who preyed on defenseless girls."

Luis chuckled. "Ah, no, my Julio has never preyed on anyone. He just likes computers and, apparently, your daughter as well."

They sat down together on a large log. The lake, glistening against the clear sky, showed no sign of the storm of the night before. Each father was lost in his own thoughts about his child. Luis remembered Julio as a ten-year-old, steering his uncle's sailboat, wearing an old sailor's cap, and grinning into the sunlight as he pretended the boat was his own. He remembered the swim meets and the band concerts, and the proud glint in his son's eye as he mastered new skills. To end all that pride and potential in a place so far from the home he loved . . . Guilt and anguish made Luis sigh and bury his head in his hands.

Cornell remembered Romi's fifth birthday, when she rode her new bike proudly with no training wheels. He smiled, remembering the look of victory on her face that day. He thought of her part in the school play when she was nine, of her face as she sang in the choir at church, of how she would look next year when she graduated from high school. He stopped himself then, afraid to think of the future. He glanced around the woods. Somewhere in this soft green space, or that dark blue space in the distance, his daughter waited for her dad to find her. He pulled a branch from the log they were sitting on and broke it in frustration. He reached down to snap another branch when a speck of blue caught the corner of his eye.

"Luis, what is that under that log behind us?" he asked, not wanting to show any excitement in his voice.

"What? I see nothing. Where is the flashlight?"

"Look, lodged under those rocks and sticks. It's a shirt—a blue-jeans shirt."

"*¡Oh, Dios mío!* I see it! Julio was wearing a shirt like that—but this one is torn, and muddy, and . . ."

"Pull it out. There's a hand! Oh, Luis, I think we've found them!" Cornell's heartbeat was like the thunder from the night before. Luis couldn't stop shaking. He could hardly grab Julio's shirt.

"*¡Dios mío!* It is my Julio! And Romiette! Together under this fallen tree by the spillway. We've been walking back and forth over this area for hours! Oh, God, she's so cold!"

"They're not dead. They're very cold, and they're unconscious. But I can feel a pulse in both of them. Hurry, send up the flare! Get the medical team over here! We have found them!" Cornell shouted to the sky in exultation.

59.

News Update

Lawrence was tired of following Nannette with the camera, not because the camera was heavy—that was his job—but because she never knew what questions to ask, and she never knew when it was time to stop talking. None of the cameramen liked being assigned to Nannette. They'd have a lottery each day, and the loser had to work with her. Today was Lawrence's day, and he hadn't even lost the lottery. He had volunteered because of his respect for Cornell Cappelle. He'd had a little break earlier while Nannette left to go change her clothes. While she was gone, he'd helped answer phones and unload equipment from the various volunteers. She had returned, however, in an outfit that looked like something someone would wear on a safari. Tall leather boots, khaki slacks and shirt, with a matching hat—still not very good for walking in the mud, but at least her pink shoes would have a chance to dry out.

He sighed when he saw her return in her red Mercedes. "You've been sitting around for an hour doing nothing," she accused him cheerfully. "Let's get back to work, Lawrence. I'm ready now." He said nothing, but shouldered his equipment and glanced back at the other volunteers who said with their eyes that they understood.

Nannette found a man serving sodas to the searchers, so she headed over to speak to him first. She didn't even ask what had happened during the search in her absence. She smoothed her hair, checked her makeup, and smiled for the camera. "This is Nannette Norris, reporting live for Channel Six from London Woods Lake. We are still searching fruitlessly for the bodies of Romiette Cappelle and Julio Montague. Hundreds of volunteers have come to assist in the search effort." She pointed the mike in the face of the soda volunteer. "Can you tell me, sir, what kinds of sodas you are serving to the volunteers here—wait, there's a commotion at the edge of the woods! I think—it looks like—they've found Romiette and Julio!"

She left the volunteer in midsentence, and ran quickly to where a crowd was gathering around Cornell Cappelle and Luis Montague. Each carried a large, heavy burden.

Nannette continued with excitement, "I can see the two fathers—each is carrying a child. Cornell Cappelle is carrying what appears to be the body of his daughter, Romiette, and Luis Montague is carrying the body of his son, Julio. It is indeed a sad day here today. Romiette Cappelle and Julio Montague have been found dead, here in London Woods. Let's have a moment of silence on this solemn occasion."

She waited exactly two seconds, then declared brightly, "I'm going to try to get closer to see if we can determine the cause of death." She tried to push her way through the crowd, but dozens of noisy, seemingly exultant people blocked her way.

Lawrence looked at the two fathers. They weren't just smiling—they were beaming with joy. He whispered to Nannette, "Pssst! Ms. Norris! They're alive!"

She glanced up at him in astonishment, looked to where the fathers were approaching, and said glibly, "Wait, one of the children seems to be moving! Hey, they're not dead! Oops! Sorry, looks like I spoke too soon—but they looked dead at first, honest. Ladies and gentlemen, we are pleased to announce that Romiette and Julio have been found and apparently . . . uh . . . at least one of them is alive!" She lowered her mike an inch, then yelled, "Hey, Lawrence, are they both alive, or is one of them dead? Oh, am I still on the air? Oops again!" Lawrence said nothing, but kept the camera rolling as Nannette blundered on.

"Sorry, folks," she blurted. "Let me get this straight for you. It looks like both Romiette Cappelle, daughter of our own TV Six anchor Cornell Cappelle, and Julio Montague, son of Luis and Maria Montague, have been found alive. Their conditions are unknown at this time, but they look pretty bad, all wet and muddy." Lawrence shook his head in disbelief.

Nannette worked her way through the crowd until she could get a closer look. With proper respect for the situation, Lawrence turned the camera away from Romiette and Julio and toward the faces of the cheering volunteers. Nannette, totally unaware, kept on talking.

"The young people are, however, seemingly unconscious, and considered critical until we get to the hospital and find out more. They are being loaded into waiting ambulances as crowds of cheering volunteers hug and congratulate each other." The two ambulances fired up their sirens and wailed off in the distance. "Ladies and gentlemen—we have much to celebrate. We will report to you live from Good Samaritan Hospital as soon as we have more news. Stay tuned to News Six."

She turned to Lawrence. "Wow! That was great! Let's get down to the hospital quick! I want to be the first to interview the parents. Cornell is a great personal friend, you know."

Lawrence, as usual, said nothing. As he loaded up his gear, he whispered a silent prayer of thanks for the safe return of Julio and Romiette.

60.

At the Hospital—8 P.M.

Julio awakened and smelled roses—lots of roses. For a moment he couldn't remember anything, only that when he tried to move, every muscle ached and his head throbbed like thunder. He sat up slowly and painfully in his hospital bed and looked around in disbelief. Dozens of bouquets of flowers, many of them roses, filled every available space. He couldn't understand why so many flowers would be here, and then he remembered. Romiette, the storm, the water, the cold, the fear. His head dropped back to the pillow, and he let Romi consume his thoughts. He prayed she was safe. He had so many questions.

His mother peeked in the door and ran to him, her arms outstretched in one of those loving hugs only a mother can give. She wept, with joy this time, as she buried her face in his hair. Julio wept also, murmuring to her, "Mama—*Lo siento,* Mama. I'm so sorry. I did not mean to make you worry."

"Sh-sh-sh! *¡Mi Julio—mi hijo!* You have nothing to apologize for. You are a hero. You have saved her. Just as she saved you."

"Romiette! Is she alive? I couldn't get her to breathe! Oh, Mama, I couldn't bear it if something had happened to her. I told you she was special, Mama."

"*Sí*," she said, smoothing his hair as soon as she ruffled it. "I remember."

Julio frowned, trying to force the memories. "I don't remember much after the boat exploded and we lost each other in the water."

His mother shuddered. "I don't know if I can bear to hear such terrible things. All I know is that the doctors say that it seems that the warmth of your bodies kept both of you alive through the cold and damp of the night. Alone, you both might have died. But together, you lived."

Julio was afraid to believe her. "Are you sure she's OK?"

"Yes, my son, she is fine. She is cold and wet and stiff, but she did not drown, thanks to you."

"I want to see her," Julio said decisively. He tried to sit up quickly, but his pounding head made him slow his movements.

"*Sí*, very soon, Julio," his mother assured him. "But first your father wants to see you. When the doctor told us you were awake, he asked the woman a million questions. He is very proud of you, Julio," she whispered as Luis walked into the room.

"*Hola*, Papa," Julio said quietly. "I am sorry I caused you so much worry."

Luis took one look at his pale and haggard son, propped on pillows and surrounded by flowers, and for the first time since the ordeal began, Luis Montague allowed himself to break down. Finally, he hugged his son and, sniffing to regain his dignity, said, "You were very foolish, Julio."

"I know, Papa," Julio admitted. "I'm sorry all this happened, but I'm not sorry about caring for Romi. I would go through it all again to make sure she was safe."

Luis sighed. "I too should apologize. I was wrong to forbid you to see her. Her parents and your mother and I spent many hours together. I have learned much."

Julio grinned. "I will do my best to obey you, Papa. I still have much to learn too."

One nurse came in to take Julio's temperature, and another brought him some soup. He thought he had never tasted anything more delicious in his life. He relaxed and told his parents all he could remember about the evening. Every few minutes he'd ask if he could see Romi. Finally Maria laughed and told him she'd make it happen. She left the room smiling.

Romi's room was just down the hall. She too awakened to a room full of flowers sent by well-wishers from all over the city. Her mother sat in a rocking chair next to the bed. Her father had been standing at the foot of her bed, watching her sleep, with love and amazement on his face.

Romi turned her head and smiled at her mother. "Am I in trouble, Mom?" she asked, her voice a raspy croak.

Lady Brianna jumped from her chair and sat on the edge of her daughter's bed. "Not anymore, Romi," she murmured softly. "How do you feel?"

"Thirsty," whispered Romi.

"That's ironic," her father said with a half laugh. "After all that water, the first thing you ask for is something to drink." He poured a small paper cup of water and fed it to her gently. "Is my princess going to be OK?" he asked her.

"I think so, Daddy. I'm sore all over, and my throat hurts, but I feel OK." She looked around the room. "Who sent all these flowers?"

"Do you know that hundreds of people have been searching the park for you?" her mother asked.

"Really?" Romi asked in genuine surprise.

"And hundreds more saw the reports on the news and sent good wishes, and prayed for you and Julio. They're just glad you're alive and well."

"Is Julio OK, Mom? It was like my dream. I was so scared, Mom."

Her mother soothed her. "He's fine, honey. Can you tell me about it?"

Romi shuddered. "The water, the storm, the lightning—I just knew I was going to die, but Julio was holding my hand. I was fine as long as I had his hand in mine, but the storm and the lightning and the fire separated us. The boat exploded; I went under the water. Oh, Mom, it was so cold, and I couldn't breathe, and then I went under again, and then it was like my dream. Julio was calling my name, and I was floating, and then it was dark, and cold, and that's all I remember. The last thing I remember was Julio's hand in mine. Where is he, Mom? I've got to see him. He wouldn't let me die. Are you sure he's OK?"

"His father told me he's going to be just fine," Cornell assured her. "He's tired and sore, as you are, and he's been asking to see you too. The doctors are going to bring him in here as soon as he's been checked out. Are you sure you feel all right?"

"Bring him in here? I look awful!" Romi threw her hands up to her hair, which was matted and uncombed.

Her mother laughed, a strong laugh of release and joy. "You nearly died last night and you're worried about your hair? That shows how well you really are!" She laughed so hard, she had to sit down. "You look beautiful to me," she said finally, "and to Julio too, I expect." Her laughter stopped suddenly as she noticed Romi's worn face on the pillow. "You're shivering, Romi," she said with concern.

"I'm cold, Mom. Can I have another blanket?" Her mother swiftly covered her, and her dad brought another blanket. "Thanks," Romi whispered from beneath the covers.

"Sure, baby. You've been through so much. We thought we had lost you," her father admitted huskily.

"I don't remember getting out of the water," Romi mused. "Julio saved me, didn't he?"

"Apparently so."

Romi smiled. "I knew he would. He loves me."

"Yes, Romi, that too is very clear."

"Mom, you know how you feel about Daddy? How you smile and cheer up when he gets home from work?"

Lady B. grinned at her husband as he winked at her. "Yes, dear, I know," she told Romi.

"Do you think about him all the time, even though you're married and stuff?"

Her parents smiled again. "All the time," her mother said.

"And you know how you send Mom flowers at work for no reason sometimes, Daddy? That must mean you're thinking about her too."

"Yes, dear, your daddy still makes me tingle inside."

"That's how I feel when I'm with Julio," Romi said simply.

"I understand, Romi," her mother said with sincerity. "I really do understand. It's clear that you and Julio have something very special."

Cornell said nothing. He wasn't quite ready to see his daughter grow up in front of him.

"It happened really fast, Mom. I never planned to fall for any guy, let alone Julio."

"That kind of stuff is never planned. That's why it's so wonderful!"

"You're not angry?" Romi asked.

"Angry? Why? Because you fell in love?" Her mother smiled.

"Because I didn't tell you about the gang stuff."

Cornell answered, "No, but I wish you had. We could have called the police and nipped this early."

"I'm sorry, Daddy, I just didn't understand how dangerous it was. Me and Julio couldn't figure out why they wanted to hurt us. Did they catch the gang kids?"

"Yes, all five of them," her father told her. "They have the car that was used to kidnap you, the guns, even Ben's videotape."

"Oh, Romi, it could have been so much worse!" her mother cried, realizing what almost happened. "They could have killed you!"

"I know, Mom," Romi said sincerely. "I will always be thankful that this day turned out the way it did. Where's Julio? I've got to see him."

"He'll be here in a moment," her mother replied. "First, I want you to meet his mother." Maria Montague had appeared at the door. "She and I have become very close. Maria, this is my daughter, Romiette." Julio's mother smiled warmly and gave Romi a big hug.

"Hello, Mrs. Montague," Romi said with no shyness at all. "I've nev~r met you, but I feel as if I know you."

"And you too, my child. I am so glad that you and Julio are safe. We have much to talk about."

"Oh, yes, ma'am," Romi answered. She liked Julio's mom right away. Maria left to return to Julio's room, and Mrs. Cappelle decided to go with her. They walked out, and immediately the door burst open again and in strolled Destiny and Ben. Romi grinned with delight.

"Hey, Romi! What it is, girlfriend!" said Destiny, trying not to show her worry and relief. She tried to lighten the air a bit by sniffing the flowers and making a face at the ones that smelled bad.

"Destiny!" Romi exclaimed. "What took you so long?"

"Hey, I been chillin' out in the woods all day—you know what I'm sayin'—nothing else to do."

Romi grinned. "How do I look, Destiny?"

Destiny got out a comb, then tossed it back into her purse in defeat. "Girlfriend, your hair is messed *up!*"

Romi laughed. "It's the natural look!" Ben hadn't said a word yet. He was overwhelmed with the flowers. He simply stared at them in amazement. "Hey, Ben," Romi teased, "speaking of hair, your hair is looking a little faded this morning."

"I may shave it all off and start over," he said seriously.

"What color is your hair, really?" Destiny asked him.

Ben thought for a moment and shrugged. "I don't know. Been so long since I've seen it. Yep, maybe it's time for Ben to try the natural look too!"

Destiny got serious. "So what happened out there, Romi?"

"Julio saved my life," Romi said simply. "He loves me, Destiny. He told me!"

"Awesome!" Destiny replied. "Adventure and love all in the same day. Truly awesome! Me and Ben have been looking for you all night long."

"Just the two of you?" Romi asked suspiciously.

"Well, we spent most of the storm in my car, but the rest of the time we were looking for you. And guess what, Romi? We got the Fantastic Five!"

"All the times from 1:11 to 5:55? I don't believe it!"

"Yeah, Ben and me wished them all—together. If I forgot, he reminded me."

"Ben reminded you? You believe in our secret wish system, Ben?"

"Hey, it worked, didn't it?"

"That's why I knew you would be safe. That, and my advanced psychic abilities," Destiny added.

"You were doubting those abilities a couple of hours ago, Destiny," Ben reminded her.

"Never! You can't prove it! It's not like you have it on tape." Destiny laughed.

"Speaking of tape, how did they find the Minicam?" Romi asked.

"It was in the trunk of Terrell's car," Ben reported with excitement. "We even got to watch part of it this morning at the boathouse—they showed it on TV! It's gonna help convict all of them, one of the cops told me."

"Wow, so we helped after all," Romi mused.

"I'm glad all what you went through was good for something," Destiny said seriously.

"Hey, Destiny," called Romi. "Come over here close to the bed. I've got something to whisper in your ear."

Destiny leaned over close to Romi's face. "Yeah, Romi. What's up?"

"You remember you said your soul mate would come from London?" whispered Romi.

"Yeah. So?" Destiny didn't follow where Romi was headed.

"Maybe your dream meant London Woods! And

wasn't he supposed to be big in music? And colors? Isn't that a perfect description of Ben?"

Destiny sat back on the bed with a thud. "Well, shut my mouth! I had my soul mate in front of me all the time? And it's Ben? I want my money back! I mean, your money back!"

"Relax, Destiny. I can tell Ben's crazy about you by the way he looks at you." Romi grinned as Destiny looked over at Ben with new eyes. She wasn't sure if she wanted Romi to be right or not. Ben looked at both girls like they were crazy.

Romi's mother came back into the room, and Romi asked, "Mom, where's Julio?"

"Perfect timing," her mother replied. "The nurses are bringing him in now. Here they come!"

Romi was suddenly quiet. "*Hola,* Julio," she said softly.

"*Hola,* Romi. Are you OK?" He looked worried.

Romi tried to smooth her hair, but with no results. "Yeah," she said, seeing no one but Julio. "I'm fine. Just fine."

"Quit grinning so wide, Romi. Your face is gonna break!" teased Destiny.

Ben looked at Julio and remarked, "Julio is just as bad. Let's get out of here, Destiny. They need a few minutes alone."

"OK, Ben," she agreed easily. "I'm gonna let you take me out to dinner!"

"Bet," he grinned. "I don't have to eat health food, do I?"

"No," teased Destiny, "but you have to watch me eat it!"

"No problem. Let's go. And just to show I believe in equal opportunity, Destiny, I'm gonna let you pay!"

"The modern gentleman!" Destiny bowed and, with great exaggeration, escorted him from the room as they both cracked up with laughter.

"Later, Ben. Later, Destiny," called Julio. Romi felt so much better, having her friends and family close by again.

Cornell had gone to get coffee while the teenagers were in the room. As Ben and Destiny left, he walked back in. He glanced at Julio, smiled slightly, and nodded in his direction.

"Daddy," Romi said, "this is Julio."

"Hello, son," Cornell said cordially. "It's been quite a ride these last two days. Are you going to be OK now?"

"Yes, sir. I am fine. It's Romiette I worry about. She was so cold, and I was afraid she'd never breathe again."

"You did a fine job, Julio. You saved her life. I can never repay you for that. She is my flower." Cornell looked at his daughter lovingly.

"Yes, sir," Julio replied, readily agreeing with him. "She is truly a flower. *¡Una flor hermosa!*"

Romi interjected, "Would you two quit talking about me like I'm dead or something!" Then she decided to cut through the delicate steps Julio would dance before he had nerve enough to ask Cornell for a job. "Daddy, Julio wants to work in the newsroom.

He wants to learn how to use the cameras and produce a news show. Is there something he can do at the station after school or during summer vacation?"

"I'm sure we can find something. That intern job is still open—the one I offered you, Romi."

"Yeah, but I hate that kind of stuff," Romi said, pretending to gag. "Julio eats it for dinner."

"I would love to have the opportunity, sir—"

"Say no more, son. How about two weeks from Monday, after school," said Cornell, checking his pocket organizer. "Stop by and we'll show you the ropes. You willing to put in long hours?"

"Oh, yes!" Julio's eyes were wide with anticipation.

"And sweep the floor if it needs it?"

"Even before you ask!" Julio promised.

"Learn the cables and the cameras?" Cornell continued.

"As fast as you can teach me!" Julio replied.

"You got the job!"

"Thank you, sir. You won't be sorry." Julio grinned.

"You're not planning to be a news anchor, are you?" teased Cornell.

"Not soon, sir. You've got a couple of years before I'm ready for *your* job!" Julio teased boldly.

Cornell grinned at Romi. "I like this kid," he said.

"Me, too, Daddy," Romi said quietly.

61.

The Six O'clock Evening News

It was one minute to airtime. The Montagues fidgeted nervously, smoothing their clothes and hair. Cornell was miked and ready, and Lawrence the cameraman sat grinning in the shadows in the back of the studio. The two families had decided that the best way to inform the community, and to thank everyone who had helped, was to go on the air live at the top of the evening news.

Julio and Romiette rested comfortably, watching the news from their hospital beds. They continued to be amazed at all the attention that their disappearance had generated. From kids at school to total strangers, everyone wanted to reach out and share the joy of their rescue. A reporter from the *Today* show had called, a film crew showed up, and Romi and Julio's interview was scheduled to air the next morning.

The red light on top of Camera One blinked. It was time.

—*Ladies and gentlemen—this is Cornell Cappelle. Standing next to* me is my wife, Lady Brianna Cappelle, and on this side are Maria and Luis Montague, our friends.

—I would like to bring you up to date on the facts as we know them right now. First of all, I would like to thank everyone—the volunteers, the searchers, the organizers, the folks who brought the doughnuts, everyone—for their help in finding my daughter, Romiette, and the Montagues' son, Julio. Such a community outpouring has been so very much appreciated. We could not have gone through this ordeal without your support, and we cannot begin to convey our deepest thanks.

—From what we can gather, Romiette and Julio had been harassed at school by some young people who may or may not have been identified with a gang. They were stopped near London Woods, grabbed and placed in a car, then taken to the boathouse near London Woods Lake. From what we can tell, it was a means to frighten and intimidate our children, and it got out of hand.

—Romiette and Julio were then tied up, put in the bottom of a small boat, and set afloat on London Woods Lake. On an ordinary day, that might not have been life-threatening, but you are all aware of the storm last night, and there is the fact that my daughter cannot swim.

—Evidently, they were able to untie the ropes that held them, but they were adrift in the boat in a storm in the dark. Lightning finally struck the boat, and it was destroyed. They were forced to jump into those frigid waters, and Romiette almost drowned. Julio managed to drag her to safety, even after she had been overcome by the force of the water and the storm.

—When they reached the shore, Julio, carrying the unconscious Romiette, apparently tripped and fell over some storm-fallen trees. Close to unconscious himself from the cold and exposure, he dragged *her to safety in a hollow under some rocks and branches lodged under a huge fallen tree. The two of them huddled there the rest of the night—both of them drifting in and out of consciousness, Julio protecting Romiette with his body. That is how we found them—huddled together—barely conscious but, praise the Lord, very much alive.*

—They are both awake, alert, and hungry. Neither seems to have suffered any major injuries, although both will probably have headaches for a few days, and Romiette had quite a bit of water in her lungs.

—Once again, let me thank our new friends, the Montagues, and our many other friends who helped in the rescue effort. It shows what a community can do when it cares about its young people. And, although I love Shakespeare, I sure am glad that this story of the Montagues and the Cappelles did not end as Shakespeare's tale did.

They cut to a commercial then, and Maria Montague let out a huge sigh of relief. They all laughed and headed to the rear of the studio. Cornell didn't have to finish the news that evening; he had been given the rest of the night off to get some much-needed rest. As they headed out to the parking lot, they passed Nannette carrying a huge box.

"Nannette, what in the world are you doing?" Cornell asked.

"I'm taking my stuffed animals home from the office. This is my third box," she replied cheerfully.

"Why?"

"Oh, didn't they tell you? I got a new job! No

more ruining designer shoes for me! I'm moving to Indianapolis, where I'm gonna have my own talk show on cable TV! I'm gonna call it *Nannette's News*. Uncle Roscoe arranged it for me after he saw my interviews today. He said he'd never seen anything like that before."

"Well, that much I can agree with," Cornell chuckled. "I wish you the best, Nannette," he said sincerely.

She turned back and continued up the steps, whistling, and never noticed Cornell's dance of joy.

62.

Phone Call—Soul Mates

Romi curled up on the sofa in the living room with a bag of chips and a book. She and Julio had been back to school for about a month. Spring was fast approaching, and Destiny was already agonizing over which dress to wear to the prom in May. The phone ringing startled her for just a second, but she picked up the receiver on the first ring.

"Hi, Romi!" Julio's voice, which always made her smile, floated to her ear. "Isn't normal wonderful!" he said.

"You got that right." Romi grinned. "To have to complain about school and homework and the taste of grape soda—how very ordinary and fine!"

"It's hard to be famous," Julio mused. "The kids at school sure treat us differently."

"Yeah, I liked it better when I was just Romi, the girl with the new orange sweater, not Romi, the girl who almost died in the lake."

"Don't sweat it. It will be over soon, and you'll be ordinary Romi once again. But you'll always be special to me."

"I guess everybody is supposed to get fifteen minutes of fame," Romi said seriously. "I'm glad we got ours together." Both were silent for a moment. "But I'm ready now to be ordinary, just go to school together, and play with Taco."

"I'm with you on that! Are we still going to the movies tonight, Romi?"

"For sure! What shall we see? Nothing with gangs or near-drownings, though, bet?" she teased.

"You got that right," agreed Julio.

Romi heard a thumping, crashing sound in the background. "What was that?" She laughed.

"Taco," Julio chuckled. "That silly puppy just ran through here—chasing a fly, I think. She knocked down a wastebasket and a chair." Romi could almost see Julio's smile through the phone. "Such a silly puppy," Julio said quietly. "I really love her. And I really love you, even though you don't chase flies!"

"I could learn, if that's what turns you on!" Romi laughed.

"No, I think I like you just the way you are, Romiette. No flies necessary."

"You know, Julio, it's hard to grab hold of all that happened to us. It really is like something from a movie."

"And I can't help thinking how close it is to the Shakespeare story—sort of," added Julio.

Romi laughed, "I don't think even Shakespeare could have imagined this one! We really managed to live through one of our crazy fantasies, Julio."

"You're right," he said seriously. "It was scary for

more than a moment, though. And it made me realize how much I care about you. I don't care what color you are, or what color your daddy is, or the color of your car or your dog. I just care about you, and the person you are. I am so glad that we are both alive so that I can tell you that."

Romi was silent for a moment. Finally she said quietly, "I feel so close to you, Julio. I don't know when your smile first became a part of mine."

"And you say I talk fancy," he teased her. "But I know what you mean. Always remember, Romi, that nothing can ever destroy the part of you that is a part of me. You are the mate of my soul. *Te amo*, Romiette."

"I love you, Julio."

"Soul mates," he said quietly.

"Forever."

A Reader's Guide
by Dr. Alexa Sandman

As the novel opens, Romiette is awakened at 3 a.m., shaken by a powerful and vivid dream. Romiette decides to write in her journal, as Draper reveals that "Writing soothed her, relaxed her . . ." Is this how you feel about writing in general? Some kinds of writing?

What is the appeal of gangs? Which character, would you argue, finds the appeal most compelling?

Granpa tells Julio, just before moving to Cincinnati, to "keep the river in [his] heart and follow it" (Chapter 4). What do you think Granpa meant?

Destiny's name fits her well. How do her actions and words support her beliefs about the world?

What can you tell about Julio by the things he unpacks in Chapter 17? How else does Draper reveal who he is?

How do you feel about Ben? Would he be a good

friend to have? Does his physical appearance influence your viewpoint? Why or why not?

Both fathers remained focused on appearances—Romiette's race and Julio's interest in the computer and the possible gang affiliation—even throughout much of the search. Why? How do the mothers differ?

Several times in the novel, the similarity of Romiette and Julio's names to those of the title characters in Shakespeare's *Romeo and Juliet* is noted. How else are Romiette and Julio's and Romeo and Juliet's lives similar? Are any other characters similar? In name or substance, or both?

Draper uses foreshadowing to anticipate the climax of the novel. What clues does she gives as the story unfolds?

Why do you suppose Nannette Norris is a part of the story? Why would Draper include her?

This novel is told in multiple text formats. What do you think Draper's purpose was in using this technique to tell the story?

Draper writes: "I learned to dream through reading, learned to create dreams through writing, and learned to develop dreams through teaching. I shall always be a dreamer." How does this apply to Romiette? What do you think Draper's dream is for Romiette and Julio?

Activities and Research Possibilities

Chapter 2 records the beginnings of Romiette's new journal. She begins by "describing who she was." Write your own journal entry, introducing yourself and your family as Romiette does.

What do you know about gangs in contemporary society? See what you can find out using the Internet, newspaper, and magazine articles. Then, using the same resources, find about about gangs in your own city.

Is the danger of meeting people over the Internet overplayed in the novel? Research actual stories of such connections. Why might your research be biased one way or the other?

Ben says, "Pink and silver hair is what poetry is all about. Expression! Creativity!" (Chapter 28) What do you think? Try to respond in a poetic format.

Compare the structure of *Romiette and Julio* with

Draper's first novel, *Tears of a Tiger*. How are the two novels similar? How are they different? What do you think Draper's purpose was in using this technique to tell her stories?

What's new from Sharon M. Draper?
Here is an excerpt from her stunning
new novel, *Copper Sun.*

IN SPITE OF THE HEAT, AMARI TREMBLED. *The buyers of slaves had arrived. She and the other women were stripped naked. Amari bit her lip, determined not to cry. But she couldn't stop herself from screaming out as her arms were wrenched behind her back and tied. A searing pain shot up through her shoulders. A white man clamped shackles on her ankles, rubbing his hands up her legs as he did. Amari tensed and tried to jerk away, but the chains were too tight. She could not hold back the tears. It was the summer of her fifteenth year, and this day she wanted to die.*

Amari shuffled in the dirt as she was led into the yard and up onto a raised wooden table, which she realized gave the people in the yard a perfect view of the women who were to be sold. She looked at the faces in the sea of pink-skinned people who stood around pointing at the captives and jabbering in their language as each of the slaves was described.

She looked for pity or even understanding but found nothing except cool stares. They looked at her as if she were a cow for sale. She saw a few white women fanning themselves and whispering in the ears of well-dressed men—their husbands, she supposed. Most of the people in the crowd were men; however, she did see a poorly dressed white girl about her own age standing near a wagon. The girl had a sullen look on her face, and she seemed to be the only person not interested in what was going on at the slave sale.

Amari looked up at a seabird flying above and remembered her little brother. I wish he could have flown that night, *Amari thought sadly.* I wish I could have flown away as well.

I. AMARI AND BESA

"WHAT ARE YOU DOING UP THERE, KWASI?" Amari asked her eight-year-old brother with a laugh. He had his legs wrapped around the trunk of the top of a coconut tree.

"For once I want to look a giraffe in the eye!" he shouted. "I wish to ask her what she has seen in her travels."

"What kind of warrior speaks to giraffes?" Amari teased. She loved listening to her brother's tales—everything was an adventure to him.

"A wise one," he replied mysteriously, "one who can see who is coming down the path to our village."

"Well, you look like a little monkey. Since you're up there, grab a coconut for Mother, but come down before you hurt yourself."

Kwasi scrambled down and tossed the coconut at his sister. "You should thank me, Amari, for my treetop adventure!" He grinned mischievously.

"Why?" she asked.

"I saw Besa walking through the forest, heading this way! I have seen how you tremble like a dove when he is near."

"You are the one who will be trembling if you do not get that coconut to Mother right away! And take her a few papayas and a pineapple as well. It will please her, and we shall have a delicious treat tonight." Amari could still smell the sweetness of the pineapple her mother had cut from its rough skin and sliced for the breakfast meal that morning.

Kwasi snatched back the coconut and ran off then, laughing and making kissing noises as he chanted, "Besa my love, Besa my love, Besa my love!" Amari pretended to chase him, but as soon as he was out of sight, she reached down into the small stream that flowed near Kwasi's tree and splashed water on her face.

Her village, Ziavi, lay just beyond the red dirt path down which Kwasi had disappeared. She headed there, walking leisurely, with just the slightest awareness of a certain new roundness to her hips and smoothness to her gait as she waited for Besa to catch up with her.

Amari loved the rusty brown dirt of Ziavi. The path, hard-packed from thousands of bare feet that had trod on it for decades, was flanked on both sides by fat, fruit-laden mango trees, the sweet smell of which always seemed to welcome her home. Ahead she could see the thatched roofs of the homes of her people, smoky cooking fires, and a chicken or two, scratching in the dirt.

She chuckled as she watched Tirza, a young woman about her own age, chasing one of her family's goats once again. That goat hated to be milked and always found a way to run off right at milking time. Tirza's mother had threatened several times to make stew of the hardheaded animal. Tirza waved at Amari, then dove after the goat, who had galloped into the undergrowth. Several of the old women, sitting in front of their huts soaking up sunshine, cackled with amusement.

To the left and apart from the other shelters in the village stood the home of the chief elder. It was larger than most, made of sturdy wood and bamboo, with thick thatch made from palm leaves making up the roof. The chief elder's two wives chattered cheerfully together as they pounded cassava fufu for his evening meal. Amari called out to them as she passed and bowed with respect.

She knew that she and her mother would soon be preparing the fufu for their own meal. She looked forward to the task—they would take turns pounding the vegetable into a wooden bowl with a stick almost as tall as Amari. Most of the time they got into such a good rhythm that her mother started tapping her feet and doing little dance steps as they worked. That always made Amari laugh.

Although Amari knew Besa was approaching, she pretended not to see him until he touched her shoulder. She turned quickly and, acting surprised, called out his name. "Besa!" Just seeing his face made her grin. He was much taller than she was, and she had to stand on tiptoe to look into his face. He had an odd little birthmark on his cheek—right at the place where his face dimpled into a smile. She thought it looked a little like a pineapple, but it disappeared as he smiled widely at the sight of her. He took her small brown hands into his large ones, and she felt as delicate as one of the little birds that Kwasi liked to catch and release.

"My lovely Amari," he greeted her. "How goes your day?" His deep voice made her tremble.

"Better, now that you are here," she replied. Amari and Besa had been formally betrothed to each other last year. They would be allowed to marry in another year. For now they simply enjoyed the mystery and pleasure of stolen moments such as this.

"I cannot stay and talk with you right now," Besa told her. "I have seen strangers in the forest, and I must tell the council of elders right away."

Amari looked intently at his face and realized he was worried. "What tribe are they from?" she asked with concern.

"I do not think the Creator made a tribe such as these creatures. They have skin the color of goat's milk." Besa frowned and ran to find the chief.

As she watched Besa rush off, an uncomfortable feeling filled Amari. The sunny pleasantness of the afternoon had suddenly turned dark. She hurried home to tell her family what she had learned. Her mother and Esi, a recently married friend, sat on the ground, spinning cotton threads for yarn. Their fingers flew as they chatted together, the pale fibers stretching and uncurling into threads for what would become kente cloth. Amari loved her tribe's design of animal figures and bold shapes. Tomorrow the women would dye the yarn, and when it was ready, her father, a master weaver, would create the strips of treasured fabric on his loom. Amari never tired of watching the magical rhythm of movement and color. Amari's mother looked up at her daughter warmly.

"You should be helping us make this yarn, my daughter," her mother chided gently.

"I'm sorry, Mother, it's just that I'd so much rather weave like father. Spinning makes my fingertips hurt." Amari had often imagined new patterns for the cloth, and longed to join the men at the long looms, but girls were forbidden to do so.

Her mother looked aghast. "Be content with woman's work, child. It is enough."

"I will help you with the dyes tomorrow," Amari promised halfheartedly. She avoided her mother's look of mild disapproval. "Besides, I was helping Kwasi gather fruit," Amari said, changing the subject.

Kwasi, sitting in the dirt trying to catch a grasshopper, looked up and said with a smirk, "I think she was more interested in making love-dove faces with Besa than making yarn with you!" When Amari reached out to grab him, he darted out of her reach, giggling.

"Your sister, even though she avoids the work, is a skilled spinner and will be a skilled wife. She needs practice in learning both, my son," their mother said with a smile. "Now disappear into the dust for a moment!" Kwasi ran off then, laughing as he chased the grasshopper, his bare feet barely skimming the dusty ground.

Amari knew her mother could tell by just the tilt of her smile or a fraction of a frown how she was feeling. "And how goes it with young Besa?" her mother asked quietly.

"Besa said that a band of unusual-looking strangers are coming this way, Mother," Amari informed her. "He seemed uneasy and went to tell the village elders."

"We must welcome our guests, then, Amari. We would never judge people simply by how they looked—that would be uncivilized," her mother told her. "Let us prepare for a celebration." Esi picked up her basket of cotton and, with a quick wave, headed home to make her own preparations.

Amari knew her mother was right and began to help her make plans for the arrival of the guests. They pounded fufu, made garden egg stew from eggplant and dried fish, and gathered more bananas, mangoes, and papayas.

"Will we have a dance and celebration for the guests, Mother?" she asked hopefully. "And Father's storytelling?"

"Your father and the rest of the elders will decide, but I'm sure the visit of such strangers will be cause for much festivity." Amari smiled with anticipation, for her mother was known as one of the most talented dancers in the Ewe tribe. Her mother continued, "Your father loves to have tales to tell and new stories to gather—this night will provide both."

Amari and her mother scurried around their small dwelling, rolling up the sleeping mats and sweeping the dirt floor with a broom made of branches. Throughout the village, the pungent smells of goat stew and peanut soup, along with waves of papaya and honeysuckle that wafted through the air, made Amari feel hungry as well as excited. The air was fragrant with hope and possibility.